PARFAIT MUTIMURA

MONEY CONDITIONING

An Antidote To Financial Illiteracy

INTRODUCTION: INTENT AND PURPOSE OF THIS BOOK

Background

Growing up in Rwanda, money was not just important to me and my family. It was everything. I grew up in a limited-resources environment where I thought about finances or the lack thereof all the time. However, my imagination on the overall subject matter did not go beyond meager financial dimensions–for as much as I could think of it, money was merely a tool for day-to-day survival. I could not imagine anything of use beyond just that. There was a time in my upbringing when I considered advanced knowledge in personal finance and management thereof to be a privilege reserved to the very few to whom life had given wealth worthy of consideration. I thought one had to be rich to even bother to substantially acquire knowledge on this subject. Also, I believed that besides those on the wealthy echelon, bankers and accountants were the ones suited for such knowledge for their profession's sake. Given that I lived on the opposite end of that spectrum—the have nots— therefore I resigned to ignorance on the money management topic.

As I grew older, and after I arrived in the United States to further my university education, finance as a subject still seemed very complicated, for all I could see were sheer numbers and technical banking and finance jargon. This also scared me into submitting this area of interest to the privileged mighty men and women of wealth and to those whose career choices were high finance. I had an interest in other, rather mundane mathematical fields. I wanted to become an actuary.

This perception, which is very much shared by millions of low and middle-class households around the world, as well as young upcoming professionals, is what leads most of us to completely resign from acquiring fundamental knowledge of day-to-day financial literacy. We submit to ignorance of financial matters, especially personal finance, and unfortunately become quite financially illiterate.

Myriad Reasons For This Book

My position and outlook changed when I launched a career in the financial services industry on Wall Street. This is when I was exposed to myriad cases of financial illiteracy among those I served. It was a rude awakening, which essentially led me to conceive the idea of ultimately writing this financial literacy book.

In my career, I first worked as an investment banker and investment advisor, then later as a hedge fund manager, not to mention advising family offices, high net worth individuals, as well as charitable foundations and foreign government agencies on strategies and policies.

During these roles, I got to have first-hand experience with how, even to those seemingly educated and sophisticated in their own right, financial literacy would sometimes be a foreign and uncomfortable topic. From the rather complex Wall Street high finance topics down to everyday personal finance fundamentals, I noticed a huge shortfall in our education system when it came down to teaching financial literacy in secondary school as well as in higher education universities to students headed for other careers than working in finance.

Ultimately, after my time working in the high-finance field, I took on a path of focusing my work on socially conscious initiatives, notably the promotion of financial literacy through the Mutimura Foundation, Inc. ("Foundation"), a nonprofit foundation that I founded in 2022. The Foundation's mission is to promote financial literacy by providing and making available educational materials focusing on day-to-day personal finance to young professionals, and moms and pops who are all striving to build their financial foundation, set financial goals and achieve them, build credit, to purchase homes, to send their children to college, to protect their assets, to plan and save for retirement, as well as to make solid estate planning decisions, living wills, and trusts, among others.

The above is the reason why, in collaboration with the Foundation, I decided to write this small financial literacy book and focus on easy-to-comprehend fundamentals relevant to everyday financial decisions that we make in our lives, whether on a small microeconomic scale or on a bit larger household and community level.

It is not a book about advanced strategies for investing in financial markets nor about other rather sophisticated high finance matters. It is a consumer financial literacy book that any given individual of all education levels may read, comprehend, and essentially practice.

Writing Style and Summary of Contents

I write this book in a one-on-one narration style in which I symbolically address my *younger self* as well as my *mom*, and my *pop* in the second person as "*you*," and occasionally I include myself in the conversation by employing "*we*." It is written in a conversational style in which I address my intended audience i.e. anyone reading this book, as if we are having a conversation face to face.

However, in order to maintain its academic intuitiveness, I use bullet points and short notes style to make sure that, as the reader, you get quick summary information, which can be easier to read and more likely to be retained. I do the best I can to avoid writing this as an academic textbook where some contents may appear to be mundane long dissertations. Rather, I maintain a short and precise guide and advisory style while making sure I provide detailed and resourceful information worthy of your time and interests.

Throughout the book, I embark on a journey to empower you with the knowledge and skills needed to make sound financial decisions in your day-to-day life. Whether you are just starting out on your financial independence journey or looking to improve your current financial situation and achieve your goals, this book will provide you with a solid foundation in financial literacy.

Money is an integral part of our lives. It affects our ability to provide for our needs, achieve our goals, and enjoy a comfortable and secure future. However, without a solid understanding of financial concepts and practices, managing money effectively can be challenging. Financial literacy is the key to taking control of your finances, avoiding financial pitfalls, and ultimately achieving sustainable financial success.

In this book, I break down common financial topics into easy-to-understand explanations. I start by introducing the basics of personal finance, covering essential concepts such as setting financial goals, budgeting, saving, and debt management. Understanding these fundamental concepts will lay the groundwork for building a strong financial future.

Moreover, I delve into the world of banking and financial institutions. I cover the different types of accounts, explain how to choose the right bank, and guide you through the process of managing your bank accounts effectively. You will learn about interest rates, fees, credit scores, and the importance of establishing a healthy financial relationship with banks.

Investing is another crucial aspect of financial literacy that I briefly explore. I introduce you to various investment options, such as stocks, bonds, mutual funds, and real estate. You learn about risk and return, diversification, and the power of compound interest. With this knowledge, you will be better equipped to make informed investment decisions and grow your wealth over time.

Lastly, I discuss the importance of planning for the future through retirement savings and insurance. I guide you in understanding retirement accounts, such as 401(k)s and IRAs, and provide insights into the benefits of insurance as a risk management and asset protection tool to protect yourself and your loved ones from unforeseen events.

Throughout this book, I provide practical tips and real-life examples to reinforce your understanding of the concepts. My aim is to make financial literacy accessible to everyone, regardless of their previous knowledge or background. By the end of this book, you will have the tools and confidence to take control of your finances, make informed financial decisions, and pave the way to a more secure and prosperous future. However, it is important to note that this book is written for informational purposes only, and should not be taken, in part or as a whole, of financial or investment advice. Should you need tailored advice regarding your personal finance and money management, I urge you to contact a professional investment advisor or a certified financial planner.

So, let's dive in and begin our quest to condition our money to proper and effective use, and to achieve financial literacy together. Thank you for embarking on this journey with me.

–Parfait Mutimura

1: GOALS AND SPENDING HABITS

1.1 Understanding Your Values

Understanding your values can help you set achievable financial goals and work towards them according to the priorities you have set. Everyone has values that shape how they prioritize time, energy, and money. Values can be anything important to every individual, ranging from other people in one's life to things and places that are important in guiding how one makes financial decisions.

Is it family? Is it health and wellness? How about charitable contributions? You should ask yourself which values are more important to you, make them your priorities, and allocate your financial commitments accordingly.

As your values evolve in time, so should your financial priorities be adjusted accordingly. Therefore, it is important to set your financial priorities with a sense of flexibility in mind so that it will be easier to adjust them should your values change. The key step here is to understand your values and why those values are important to you. This will allow you to set short-term and long-term goals while making sure that your goals are aligned with your defined core values.

1.2 Goals and Money

Everyone strives for some kind of goal in his/her life. Some of us have those goals clearly and narrowly defined and written down, while others have them in a broader sense. You should ask yourself: what kind of future do I want? What are my hopes and dreams, and how do I get to them?

Goals are our desired results. It is very important to set financial goals in our lives as blueprint roadmaps to help us make choices on how we spend money.

Our goals should be specific and clear enough to help us prioritize how we use our money. We should be able to measure them and track our progress depending on the timeframe we have given ourselves in setting our goals.

The following are the five key elements that our financial goals should have in order to make sure they are properly set and have an increased likelihood of being achieved. The acronym reads **SMART**: Specific, Measurable, Action-oriented, **R**eachable, and **T**ime-bound.

Specific: Our financial goals should be specific. For example, one may say, "I want to be successful." This is not a specific goal. It is vague and subject to interpretation. A specific goal should read, "I want to buy or to build a home." As long as you have not bought a home nor built one yet, your goal has not been achieved. Therefore, setting specific goals comes with accountability because you have defined a specific performance metric against which your progress in achieving your goal is to be laid. It is very important to maintain an element of accountability stemming from setting specific goals.

Measurable: Our financial goals should also be measurable. For example, "I want to buy a five-bedroom home." Or, "I want to buy a one hundred thousand dollar

($100,000) home." Or, "I want to save $10,000 for an emergency." There has to be a way to measure or quantify our goals so that if we fall short of achieving them, we will be able to hold ourselves accountable.

So, ask yourself; are your goals specific? What exactly do you want to accomplish? Why is it important to you? Is it something you truly want enough to work hard for or is it just some nonchalant wishful thinking?

Are your goals measurable? If it is saving for your child's college, for example, decide how much money you are targeting to have earmarked for that purpose. This allows you to track progress and ultimately know whether or not you have achieved your goal.

Action-oriented: Our goal must be action-oriented. We should know what specific actions we need to take and complete in order to meet our goals. If it is earning a big salary, then you'd better work hard and long hours, and/or be smart to earn a big salary. Is it leading to a very lucrative career in sports or performance arts? Then you'd better practice your sport or routines every day if you want to stand out, be great, and be successful.

Reachable/Realistic: Our goals must be reachable/realistic. Nothing is more counterproductive than setting goals that are not realistic and reachable. Big dreams are encouraged, but make sure they remain within the realm of reality and possibilities. Ask yourself, is your goal realistically likely to be achievable considering other elements?

As much as we do get amped up by those pep talks and motivational speeches that we see on TV, it is very important to be realistic and sometimes take baby steps as we grow. When we set very unrealistic goals, we may fail, not because we are not competent, but because the goals we set couldn't be achieved given other elements beyond the realm of our influence. Unfortunately, when this happens, it can have a long-term toll on your confidence, once you see a long list of what seems to be throngs of failed causes.

Time-bound: Timeline is very important when it comes to setting financial goals, or any goal for that matter. When setting goals, we need to set a timeline to achieve them. For example, when will you buy a house? Or, if your financial goal was to have a million dollars in your bank account by the time you turned thirty years old, then today, on your thirtieth birthday, can you look at your bank account and see at least a million dollars? If that is the case, you have achieved your goal. Otherwise, even if you make five million at just thirty-one, you still did not achieved your goal set for your thirtieth birthday. This is very different from just saving as much as you can without having a specific amount in mind, set within a specific time horizon. Stating that you want to become a millionaire is not in itself a goal because this untimed goal can be stretched for a whole lifetime without ever being reached. Give yourself a specific timeframe by which your stated goal must be achieved.

So, is your financial goal time-bound?

Before you move on to the next section of this chapter, sit down and review your financial position. Write down all of your financial goals, and ask yourself: are your goals specific, measurable, action-oriented, reachable, and time-bound? If your answer is YES to all of the above questions, then you are on the right track to achieving your goals.

Buckle up.

1.3 Consumer Influences

In behavioral economics, we are taught that every financial decision we make is driven either by a **need** or a **want**; and sometimes by an **obligation**. Our needs tend to be fundamental and driven by nature and survival necessity. For example, when we look at the Maslow pyramid of needs, we see that things like food, shelter, clothing, and transportation among others are part of our day-to-day needs. Therefore, we almost always must spend money on them because we cannot lead a healthy life without them.

However, we also spend a lot of money on our wants. These are things that we desire to have but that we can actually live without. For example, we all need to eat in order to survive. Therefore spending money on food is a necessity. But we also want to wine and dine out in nice restaurants with our families and friends. This is a want. Our hearts desire to do so, but we can survive if we don't go out for wine and dinner.

Our wants are most of the time, if not always, driven by external influences, which impact our financial choices. Unless we have strategies and fortitude to curb our urges and stay focused on our financial goals, we will probably spend money on all kinds of unneeded purchases, driven by external influences.

Beware of Subliminal Messages in Ads

When we see advertisements on television, social media, or billboards, besides the obvious script or images we see, there are very powerful subliminal messages embedded in those ads. And those subliminal messages have a great impact on us because we are not conscious of them and they slowly condition our thoughts.

Unless we are careful and pay attention, we don't even stand a chance against the most obvious advertising efforts that we are constantly exposed to. When we see certain products, we instantly feel a sense of curiosity and sheer want to try them, and that is the first step to ultimately purchasing them. For example, my current iPhone 14 Pro is perfect. It is arguably the best telephone gadget on the market right now. However, when the iPhone 15 comes out, it is likely that I will see it advertised as a game changer, and I may start feeling a subliminal urge to check it out, even when my 14 Pro still works perfectly fine. This will create a want that would take a bit of willpower to curb or else fall victim to it and head to the Apple store.

Everything we see in the media, product reviews on internet platforms such as YouTube, social media, and even print advertisements are all designed to create a sense of want for new things and instill a fear of 'missing out,' not to mention a certain level of dissatisfaction with our existing situation. Advertisements are designed to instill in us a state of endless consumerism.

Celebrity Influencers

Besides general cable television, billboard, or social media advertising, celebrities make up a very effective niche of influencers. For example, a pair of sneakers worn by or named after a star athlete would command a much higher price tag. There is an element of influence in purchasing a pair of shoes worn by a household name celebrity and we need to be rationally aware of it.

This is why Nike for example, as well as other sportswear brands, pay millions of dollars to their celebrity endorsements; they understand how those celebrity influencers will help sell their products to a mass market.

Keeping Up With The Jones

Another very remarkable set of external influencers is that of peers and friends. We are more likely to buy the same things our friends have. Therefore, it is very important for us to have very strict financial plans and goals, and stick to them if we truly want to achieve them. We should not let these external influences persuade us into spending money that should be earmarked for achieving our goals.

I agree that there is nothing wrong with wanting certain things that are not necessary every once in a while, but if those things handicap any progress made toward achieving our long-term goals, then they can wait. We must learn how to delay our pleasures and curb our urges.

However, not all influences are bad. In fact, some of them may contribute to achieving your financial goals much faster. I call them **constructive influences** that can sometimes render us more inspired and hence make us very productive and high performers. They can help us achieve our goals. For example, there have been times when I incorporated other people's methods, lifestyles, and good habits. Over the course of my life, I have noticed that some positive influences have made significant contributions toward my personal growth and career.

Therefore, as I discuss external influences, it is important to accept that peer pressure and or advertisements are part of our lives and we cannot totally withdraw ourselves from them. That would be unhealthy. It is human nature to want what others have or be attracted to what we see. It is embedded in our psyche. The goal here is to find the middle. Therefore be able to maintain a healthy balance while you make consistent strides towards your goals.

It is important to know which ones are our **individual impulses** that may influence our spending habits. In order for us to stay focused, we must recognize tactics used by advertisers whether they are obvious messages or subliminal. Ask yourself; is there a friend who has tendencies to lure you into spending habits inconsistent with your set financial goals? If so, find a healthy solution for that. Maybe it is time you have a conversation with your friend about the lifestyle you are comfortable with leading, and find the balance without necessarily affecting the relationship.

Time is Money

It is also important to quantify the cost of each purchase in terms of time. Yes, time is money. Whenever you are tempted to buy an item, think about your hourly or monthly wage then divide the cost of the item by that amount to come up with how much time of work it takes you to earn enough money to buy such an item. How many hours, days, weeks, or months do you need to work in order to buy such an item, considering your earnings? Is it worth it?

The approach of quantifying the cost of purchases in terms of time has proven to be a very effective tool for people to think twice before they indulge themselves in unnecessary and costly purchases. If you have to go to work for weeks or months in order to afford a particular purchase, it better be a worthy purchase indeed.

Therefore, it is important to bear in mind how external influences impact our financial choices and decision-making process; and to use the above strategies and awareness to make sure we do not go astray from our stated financial goals.

2: BANKING FUNDAMENTALS

2.1 Financial Products, Services, And Providers

You are consumers of financial products and services, and therefore it is important to know what kind of services and products are available for you to choose from, as well as who are the providers. There are different types of financial institutions that provide a wide range of financial products and services for retail banking consumers. These financial institutions are in the business of serving different customers consistent with their intended niche. Therefore, each customizes its product and service offerings to appeal to its intended customer demographic. Most of the time, financial institutions' characteristics may appear overlapped and therefore it is not easy to tell the difference between them.

Below are some of the mainstream categories of financial institutions to know about. Those include national and regional **banks**, **savings associations**, as well as **credit unions**. These financial institutions provide similar services to their customers, with differentiation being mostly in accessibility and size of transactions.

- They accept deposits and withdrawals of money.

- They are in the money lending business.

- They may offer other financial products and services such as credit cards, car loans, personal loans, and mortgages, among others.

There are key differences between banks and credit unions. These differences make them stand out in the eyes of different customer demographics depending on the way they are structured. For example:

- Banks have customers while credit unions have members.

- Banks usually have no membership criteria, while credit unions have membership criteria.

- Banks are mostly owned by many shareholders, whether private or public ownership, while credit unions are almost always not-for-profit organizations, owned by members.

- Banks have deposit insurance. In the USA, the Federal Deposit Insurance Corporation (FDIC) protects funds depositors placed in federally insured banks in case of bank failure.

- As of 2024, the FDIC provides insurance up to at least two hundred and fifty thousand dollars ($250,000) per depositor, per FDIC-insured bank, and per ownership category.

- The National Credit Union Administration (NCUA) is the FDIC equivalent for credit unions in the USA.

- The NCUA protects funds depositors placed in federally insured credit unions.

- The insurance rules are similar to those of FDIC.

Financial institutions such as banks and credit unions do everything they can to ensure their customers or members can access their services conveniently. Services are accessed through retail locations, automated teller machines (ATMs), customer service phone numbers and contact emails, websites, as well as mobile banking and applications.

Products Offering

Each product and service offered by a financial institution is designed to offer a solution for a different customer need. Therefore, it is important to be familiar with diverse products and services offered by financial institutions so that you may decide which products or services are better suited to your current financial circumstances and your defined financial goals.

Banks and credit unions offer three (3) main categories of financial products and services available to their customers.

- In the **deposit products** category, we have savings accounts, checking accounts, certificates of deposits, and money market accounts, among others.

- In the **credit products** category, we see credit cards, lines of credit, installment loans, car loans, mortgages, and other types of privately structured debts.

- There are also other products and services including check cashing, money order retail, prepaid cards, debit cards, cashier's checks, automated teller machines (ATM), bill paying services, peer-to-peer payments, and foreign remittances transfers.

- Besides banks and credit unions, however, we also see other financial services providers such as convenience stores and United States postal services, privately owned mom-and-pop stores that sell prepaid cards, check-cashing outlets, payday lenders, vehicle title lenders, and pawn shops, not to mention merchants cash advance (MCA) boutiques, which lend to small businesses against future revenue receivables.

It is important to know what financial products and services best suit your financial goals, and decide which one to use in order to save money, spend money, manage money, or borrow. It all depends on your needs and objectives.

Now how do you decide which financial institutions are right for you? There are a number of needs that would help you decide whether a bank, credit union, or other financial institution is the right fit for you. You should ask yourself some questions such as:

- Is your primary goal to save money for emergencies?

- Is it to pay bills in a safe and secure way?

- Is it to send money to family or friends electronically? If so, is the transfer domestic or international, and what are the fees?

- Is the goal to get access to cash quickly or to borrow money?

- How about improving and/or building your credit?

It is also important to see value in building a relationship with one particular financial institution. You must sit down and decide what is your primary objective and financial need in order to help choose the right financial services provider for you.

2.2 Opening An Account

Now you have decided which financial institution best suits your goals and are asking yourself about the next step. I say the next step is to open an account with the institution of your choice. There are several reasons and advantages to opening an account with a financial institution. Some of those advantages include the following but are not limited to

- ensured safety and security from federal deposit insurance for your money placed in the bank

- earning interest on deposits depending on the account type

- convenience in paying bills or making transfers to family and friends

- building a relationship with a financial institution

In order to open an account at a financial institution, there are key elements and steps that you must take.

- The first is to complete an application for the account.

- Verify you are who you say you are. Here banks will ask for at least one or two pieces of identification such as a Driver's License, national ID, passport, military identification, date of birth, and social security number in the USA.

- Once the account is open, the bank may require that you make the first deposit in order to activate the account; this is also a part of the account opening process.

- Obviously there will be disclosures and documents which you will be required to sign.

- Everyone is not always approved for an account. It is important to maintain a good banking history because if you have a negative banking history, it may cause denial from opening any bank account in the future with the same financial institution or others.

- Negative banking history reports include unpaid negative balances on the account, suspected fraud related to accounts, and certain accounts closed by financial institutions due to failure to honor the account terms and conditions.

- Everyone has a right to a free banking history report by contacting one of the nationwide consumer reporting companies, at least once every twelve months.

- Should there be incorrect information on your banking history report, it is recommended that you file a dispute with a consumer reporting company such as Chex Systems either by mail or by going to their website and following instructions.

- Consumer reporting companies generally have 30 days to investigate the dispute on your banking history report and provide a response.

In case one has a negative banking history, some banks offer a **"second chance"** checking account. These accounts may have special fees and rules. It is important to carefully review those fees and rules to make sure that you stay current as you build a positive history. This will ultimately allow you to graduate to a regular account in the future.

What to Consider

There are a number of options you should consider in case you fall in the category of those struggling to get started:

- In the case of not having enough money to start or the maintenance fees on the accounts seem too high, you should consider low-cost accounts options available at your financial institution.

- In the case of negative information in your banking history report, please consider the "second chance" checking account for the time being.

- In the case of negative information on your credit report and low credit scores, consider various options available in credit building loans, secured credit cards, and or credit counseling.

It is important to know the general process for opening a savings or checking account, including second-chance options if you are initially unable to open a regular account.

2.3 Account Management

The way you manage your account activities depends on the purpose of your account and the financial goals you've set for that account.

Savings accounts, for example, are meant to build savings by depositing money and keeping it there to earn interest and take advantage of the wonders of compounding.

Below are highlights that characterize savings accounts:

- They are designed to save money for the future in general, or for a particular financial goal.

- They often offer higher interest rates than interest checking accounts, which are also provided by some financial institutions.

- Savings accounts are not designed for high numbers of day-to-day transactions. Some financial institutions will set a limit on how many withdrawals you can take from savings accounts each month.

Your Responsibility

In order to better manage activities in your savings accounts, and help achieve your savings goal, here are some important steps:

- Read the rules of your account and do the best you can to abide by them. Make sure you understand the fees, as well as penalties, if any, for going below the minimum daily balance or making too many transactions from the account.

- Keep track of your deposit and withdrawal. You can maintain your own entry record each time you do a transaction. There are also several applications that allow people to keep track of their transactions, linked to their bank account. Or you can use a paper-based log.

- Carefully review your account statements. Most account statements are sent on a monthly or quarterly basis, but they also can be viewed directly online. Make sure the transactions reflected on your bank statements match what you have recorded in your personal log so that you can detect suspicious activities or fraud on your account.

Checking accounts are built a bit differently, and managing them effectively is even more important because these are your everyday spending accounts. There are more transactions, deposits, withdrawals, payroll, and other cash flows coming in and out of your checking account. Therefore, these accounts are more prone to fraud or mismanagement than savings.

- Checking accounts are used for deposits, paying bills, making purchases, and accessing cash.

- They are linked to ATM cards and debit cards where money is taken directly from your accounts.

- Checking accounts allow you to obtain a checkbook and write checks against the account. The checks tell your financial institution to pay money to someone else. However, some checking accounts do not use checks. So if check writing is important to you, make sure the checking account you open allows check writing privileges.

Overdraft Fees

Checking accounts are more prone to overdraft fees. With an overdraft, the transaction goes through, cleared by your financial institution, but there is not enough money in the account to cover the transaction.

Keep an eye on the fee. Most banks, with the exception of a few special checking accounts or overdraft protection features, charge a fee for overdraft transactions. These fees do add up the more this happens to you. Keep an eye on those fees, or make sure you always have enough money in the account before you authorize a transaction or write a check.

Only financial institutions get to decide if they will cover checks or other payments that would cause an overdraft fee if processed.

Once the transaction is covered, you should expect to be charged a fee, usually $35 in most US banks. If a transaction is not covered, expect to be charged a non-sufficient funds fee, and possibly a return check fee, because that check is going to bounce.

Other Bank Features

- Banks also offer direct deposit features on most checking accounts. Direct deposit facilitates depositing money safely and securely into your bank account electronically.

- There is no need to make a deposit in person.

- Many employers offer direct deposit for their employees' payroll and also allow you to have part of your paycheck directly deposited into your savings account.

- Checking accounts also facilitate automatic bill payment, which allows you to schedule and send payments through your financial institution. Payments can be one-time or recurring.

- There is also automatic debit, which gives permission to merchants or lenders to take payments from your account. Always make sure you have enough money in your account to cover these payments.

There are many more ways to effectively manage your checking account among which include:

- making sure you review your account statements

- keeping track of holds on your debit cards and reporting them to your financial institution immediately in case the card is lost or stolen

- setting up email or text alerts

- linking your checking account to your savings account or line of credit

Another account management option you must pay attention to, if it applies to you, is the **Peer-To-Peer (P2P)** payment. The P2P, which is a money transfer to another person, helps with everyday money transactions between individuals such as paying a babysitter or splitting a taxi fare, among others.

It is a rapidly changing area of financial services, and keep in mind federal deposit insurance, fees, privacy, and funds availability, among others.

There are also **mobile wallet** applications that allow you to make point-of-sale (POS) purchases with your mobile device instead of debit, credit, or prepaid card. Always make sure that you keep your device and information secure by using hard-to-guess passwords.

In conclusion, in order to better manage your financial account and your money, learn the rules of your account and keep track of how you use it. This will help keep costs down, develop a positive banking relationship, and most importantly help achieve your banking goals.

2.4 Prepaid Cards

Now let's dive into the fast-growing world of prepaid cards. They have become the go-to tools for some consumers to securely carry money, pay bills, and partially be banked where traditional banking services are not widely available.

Below is some information that you need to know about some features of prepaid cards:

- Prepaid cards are a rapidly growing alternative to carrying cash. They are not linked to a checking or savings account.

- The money is loaded onto the card either in person, by phone, online, or through a mobile app.

- The card must be activated and registered in order to take advantage of all features.

- There are several kinds of prepaid cards including, but not limited to, reloadable prepaid cards available in most major stores such as Walmart or check cashing outlets, payroll cards, electronic benefit transfers (EBT) cards in the USA, college or university identification cards, prepaid cards for specific stores, gifts cards, et cetera.

Most reloadable prepaid cards can be used in restaurants, to withdraw cash from an ATM, or to buy groceries. They come with certain fees such as an account or card reload fee, ATM withdrawal fee, lost or stolen card replacement fee, et cetera.

The key difference between **reloadable** and **debit** cards are the following:

Reloadable Cards

- They are not linked to an account at a financial institution. So if you are unable to open an account at a bank for any reason, a reloadable prepaid card can be a good fit for you.

- The balance on a reloadable card may be insured by FDIC if certain conditions are met.

- They are safer than carrying cash, and generally cannot allow you to spend more than there is loaded on the card.

Debit cards

- They are linked directly to your checking account at a financial institution.

- You must have an account in order to have access to a debit card.

- Deposits at a federally insured financial institution are insured by FDIC (banks) or NCUA (credit union), therefore money on debit cards is also insured.

- Debit cards use money that has been deposited to your account.

- They are safer than carrying cash, and for an overdraft fee

- They may allow you to spend more than there is available on the account if you opt-in to an overdraft program.

Loss of Prepaid Card

It is important to immediately report loss, theft, or any charge you did not make to the prepaid card issuer. Protection depends on the type of the card, and you generally must register the card to make sure you get the protection offered by the card issuer.

In conclusion, always remember that prepaid cards allow you to spend or access money loaded onto them. They are usually not linked to a checking or savings account. And make sure you review their features and have them registered before you use them.

3: PERSONAL INCOME AND

EXPENSES

3.1 Income

Understanding your income is the first step to using it effectively and efficiently to meet your needs and help you achieve your financial goals. Income is simply defined as the money you receive either as a one-time income or a regular cash flow.

Types of Income

There are several types of income you can receive, including but not limited to

- **Earned income:** This is the money you earn through employment either as an employee, as an independent contractor, or from running a business. With this type of income, you must actively work for it.

- **Passive income or residual income**: This is an income from assets or investments. As the name says, it is a passive income because once you have established the mechanism for it, you don't necessarily have to actively go to work every day for it. This is usually a result of invested capital, and intellectual capital, especially in creative arts where royalties are paid.

- **Public benefits or entitlements**: These are money paid to you, such as social security, supplemental income, and other benefits from government or other welfare services, and other entitlements such as settlement payments.

Income is classified into at least two segments/categories. There is gross income and net income.

- **Gross** income is defined as the total income received without any deductions. Our salaries are usually quoted in gross terms, before tax and deductions.

- **Net** income is the remainder of gross income after deductions such as social security, pension, and tax payments.

Gross Income - Deductions = Net Income

Ways To Receive Income

There are several ways to receive income, such as cash income, paper check, direct deposit into the bank, payroll card, and electronic benefit transfer (EBT) among others.

You should select whatever option is the most convenient for you, and helps you to meet your overall financial goals.

It is important for you to understand your pay statement. Your typical pay statement will reflect the following information but is not limited to:

- your personal information

- pay period

- pay date

- gross pay amount

- deductions, if any

- net pay, and

- employer contributions to your pay or pension if any

Pay Deductions

There are two types of deductions typically reflected on your income statement. There are required deductions and elective deductions.

Required deductions, as the name says, are required. They must be deducted from your gross unless you and your employer choose to not be compliant with payroll or income tax laws. This act would be a crime.

- The Federal Insurance Contributions Act (FICA) deductions reflect your contribution to social security and Medicare insurance.

- Income tax deductions are the money taken from your paycheck so that they can be remitted to the federal, state, or local income tax collection agency. In the USA, the Internal Revenue Service (IRS) collects federal income received.

Elective deductions, however, are optional. Although they are usually recommended, one can opt out of them. These deductions are usually for insurance premiums, union membership dues, retirement accounts, contributions such as 401(k), and charitable contributions, among others.

You should understand how your income tax withholding affects your deductions and therefore your ultimate take-home pay.

Bear in mind the following:

- If you have fewer allowances, then there will be higher tax withholding, which will make your take-home income even smaller.

- The more allowances you declare on your W-4 form, the lower your tax withholding and the higher your take-home income.

- As tempting as the above sounds, you don't want to have too little withheld because then you might end up owing more tax to the government at the end of your annual tax return filings.

- Try to strike a balance between the number of allowances and the amount of take-home income.

Employment Income Categories

It is recommended that you understand how your employer categorizes you as far as payroll and tax withholding are concerned.

- If your employer gives you a W-2 IRS form, this means that you are considered an employee of the company, and most likely your employer will withhold the tax deductions from your gross pay.

- If you receive a 1099-MISC IRS form, the employer considers you a self-employed independent contractor. In this case, you are responsible for paying taxes yourself. Your client or employer will pay you gross income before any deductions, then you will need to save an estimated portion of the income for future tax payments.

- It is important for you to keep accurate records.

Tracking Your Income

You should be able to track your income so that you can be able to properly manage your money, make an accurate budget, and take on the right proportion of financial obligations taking into account your income tracker.

Regular income is an income that you receive on a regular basis such as wages or public benefits. The frequency may be weekly, bi-weekly, monthly, or even quarterly.

Unpredictable income is a type of income that you cannot rely on in the long run because it is hard, if not impossible, to tell when the next round will come in. For example, a lottery winning or gambling proceeds, to name a couple.

Seasonal income is a type of income that comes predictably on a seasonal basis. For example, the cash gift from your uncle on your birthday, every year, is one of those. An expected Christmas gift card is another example.

Finally, there is **one-time** income. This is a cash payout you get once and that is all. For example, an insurance payout after a car accident or a death. A lawsuit settlement is another example.

3.2 Expenses

Your ability to understand your expenses and details of where your money goes will help you decide how to save, share, and spend your income, along with any other financial goals. There are three ways to think about expenses. First, your **needs** are the things you must have. Second, your **wants** are the things you desire to have but can live on without. Third, your **obligations** are the debt or other payments you owe. They are your dues and must be paid for.

Before you spend, always ask yourself.

- Can you find less expensive ways to meet your needs and therefore save more?

- Can you use less money for the wants that you desire without breaking the bank?

- Can you negotiate lower payments or better payment terms on some of your obligations?

It is very important to keep in mind the following elements because they allow you to manage your expenses effectively, and therefore make strides toward achieving your financial goals:

- If you receive **public benefits** such as welfare checks, you should learn about resources and asset limits. You should monitor how your spending and savings affect countable assets based on what your next public benefit calculation is going to be. You should use income in ways that avoid exceeding asset limits that could disqualify you from your benefits.

- Your ability to track your spending habits will help you understand if you are using your money according to your values and goals. It will also help you uncover where you can make changes, while you strive to spend as little as possible.

- Your ability to manage your expenses effectively helps you avoid **late fees**, interest on unpaid balance in the case of credit card debts, negative credit reports, entries on your credit history, loss of services in case of excessive late payments or no payment at all on utilities, and additional charges associated with services reactivation.

- You should establish convenient and reliable ways to stay on top of your bills and pay them on time. You may pay them in person, the old-fashioned way, or you can pay them by mail, electronically through a financial institution, credit card, website, or subscribe to bill-paying services.

- There is also a big surge of reliable and cost-effective bill-payment apps.

3.3 Budgeting

Regardless of the size of your income, budgeting is a very crucial element of financial management. Leading a lifestyle beyond your means is the most disastrous way to end up in financial ruin. Therefore, knowing what your needs, wants, and obligations are, allows you to set a budget for them in consideration of your other long-term financial goals.

Budgeting is one of the most important building blocks to improve your financial situation.

What To Keep In Mind:

- You must know your total monthly income, which includes wages, salary, bonus, government benefits (such as social security and food assistance), child support/alimony, interest income from investment, support from family or friends, et cetera.

- You must have a detailed breakdown of your monthly expenses including housing and utilities, loans and credit cards, savings and investing, transportation, family and pets, health and grooming, food, clothing and entertainment, and miscellaneous expenses.

- For non-monthly expenses such as seasonal, quarterly, or annual bills, divide by 12 to break them down to a monthly basis.

- Label each expense as a **need**, a **want,** or an **obligation**.

- If your needs and obligations exceed your income, you need to find ways to increase your income.

- If your wants seem high, you can work on cutting them down, changing your lifestyle, or increasing your income.

Your total income minus total expenses must be positive. The remainder is your monthly disposable income that you may use to decide whether to increase savings, add a new want, donate to charity more, or invest more to build wealth and legacy.

Being able to use all of the above tools will allow you to effectively manage your income and expenses, which are important skills to achieve your stated intermediate or long term financial goals. Should you need professional assistance in this matter, you can consult a financial advisor or some nonprofit financial counseling organizations in your area.

4: SPENDING AND SAVING PLAN

It is important for you to bear in mind that having a monthly spending and saving plan is highly recommended. Not only should you have such a plan, but you must strive to stick to it in order to effectively manage your money and achieve your goals.

The first step is to compare your income and expenses as we covered earlier. You need to understand where your money is going and be able to make adjustments, as circumstances call for it.

The following are some important points to consider right at the get-go:

- If you receive income or pay expenses on a schedule other than monthly, then you will need to do the math to bring your planning up or down to monthly terms in order to better manage your planning log. Both income and expenses must be logged with the same frequency i.e. weekly, monthly, annually.

- Remember, your available income is the **net income** not **gross**. That is what you have available for you to spend.

- As you make a comparison of your income and expenses, subtract your total expenses from your income.

- If the difference is **zero** and your income equals your expenses, then you have a lot of work to do. You need to either cut down on expenses or increase your earnings.

- If the difference is **positive**, you are on the right track because your income is higher than your expenses. Now find ways to increase your income even higher while maintaining your current expense level, or reduce them if there is room for it.

- Should the difference be **negative**, however, your expenses outweigh your income. Take a hard look at your wants and see if you can cut out some of them. See if you can negotiate and pay less on your obligations, and most importantly you have to increase your income.

- Go over your receipts to track your expenses and see if there are any **promotions** or **voucher coupons** printed on your receipts to help you save.

- At least once per month, conduct a monthly financial review, have a monthly goal-setting session, and celebrate success where a celebration is due.

It is important to find ways to increase your income, which helps cover your expenses and/or save more. You can sell a few things that you own but do not need, get an ongoing part-time job or side hustle of your own, and invest in long-term **workforce development** by getting more education and **career advancement** training.

Look for ways to decrease expenses by either getting better pricing power on your **needs** and/or eliminating some of your **wants** expenses.

Tips To Decrease Expenses

- **Conserve:** With this method, you can shop cheaper or buy less. When you are shopping for goods and services, look for similar or alternate options that would equally meet your intended goal, and yet cost less for your pocket.

- **Adjust**: Ask yourself this question. What can you renegotiate? Do you have an existing lifestyle and it is costing you more than you can afford? Try to make adjustments to your existing lifestyle by, for example, reducing your membership fees down to a less expensive package. Or, move out of an expensive apartment building to a less expensive one with fewer amenities. Renegotiate with yourself or other stakeholders on what you can or cannot maintain moving forward, adjusted for your new financial goals.

- **Do without**: What can you eliminate? If you really do not need it or can do just fine without it, it is recommended that you eliminate it from your budget, especially if maintaining it hinders progress toward your own goals.

When Money Is Short

When money is short, prioritize which bills to pay first and which ones can wait a little longer. Even with careful planning, money can run short sometimes. Try to:

- increase your income in the meantime

- decrease expenses

- contact your creditors

- reach out for help

- prioritize what to pay first

When it comes to **prioritizing**, think about what can happen when a choice is made. For bills, make choices about which bills to pay in full, pay partially, or pay late. Pay attention to consequences that:

- prevent you from earning income; for example, if not paying your car insurance may prevent you from going to work and earning income, then think twice before skipping on this expense

- jeopardize your shelter such as leading to eviction from your home rental or foreclosure on your purchased home

- impact health or ability to live independently

- could result in loss of your assets, among others

In conclusion, it is important to understand the diverse nature of your expenses and categorize them in order of priority. It is also recommended to make some adjustments and/or cut some expenses completely when circumstances call for it because this will free up some disposable income to be earmarked toward your long-term financial goals. When it comes to prioritizing bill payments, give priority to the ones that would result in more consequential negative outcomes should they not be paid in a timely fashion.

5: SAVINGS PRACTICES

5.1 What is Savings

Savings is money set aside today, for the future. I must note that spending less money is not the same as saving. To build savings, you must spend less money, and systematically put some or all of what you didn't spend into savings.

Reasons To Save

There are several reasons for saving money depending on individual goals. The most common reasons people save money are for certain specific goals such as:

- buying a new home

- paying for college

- building long-term wealth

- being better prepared for future times with less income or more expenses

- having peace of mind stemming from financial security

Tips To Saving Money

There are a few quick lifestyle tips to save money as you go. The following are some examples that, if done systematically, would help you build sustainable saving habits and ultimately lead to accumulating a considerable sum in your savings account:

- Ask your financial institution what ATMs you can use without paying a fee. ATM fees seem small but they add up over time.

- Save those fees which you, otherwise, were paying.

- Shop around and open a free or low-cost checking account at a financial institution.

- If you save money, perhaps by not paying fees to cash checks, then put that money into savings.

- Before you buy something, consider whether you are paying more money only to get the brand name. It may be worth the extra cost, but sometimes a different brand or generic item can be just as good, or even better. If you spend less on it, add it to your savings.

- Set aside some money, every time you get income. Regularly saving money, even if only a small amount, can make a big difference over time.

5.2 Where To Build Your Savings

There are many options to save money, and each one has advantages and disadvantages. Consider the options that are aligned with your financial goals.

Option One: Home Safe or Lockbox

You can save money at home in a safe or a lockbox. With this option, *advantages* are that there are no fees, no rules, no additional cost to maintain, and it's very convenient and easy to access. *Disadvantages* are that money can be lost or stolen with no insurance and can be destroyed in fire, flood, or other disaster. And, it's easy to access and hence easy to spend.

Option Two: Friends and Family

Save money by having friends or family keep it for you. The *advantages* are that there is no fee, no maintenance, it may be convenient, et cetera. The *downside* is that, just like in option one, money can be lost or stolen, can be destroyed in a fire, flood, or other disaster, and most unfortunately, it may strain relationships if something happens to the money.

Option Three: Prepaid Cards

You can save money regularly with a Prepaid Card. The *advantages* are that it is easy to access, has electronic online functionalities, it's convenient, and you may be able to directly deposit wages onto the card and automatically move funds from the card to savings.

The *disadvantages* are that you have to pay fees, and the card can be stolen or lost. Please review card agreements to find out if you are protected from loss or theft. The card might not have federal deposit insurance, it might not be possible to easily move money into savings, and the card might have an expiration date.

Option Four: Rotating Savings and Credit Associations

The *advantages* here are that there is a commitment to the credit association to save on schedule, the money is not easily accessible until it is your scheduled turn to receive a lump sum, and you get the lump sum at a known date.

The *disadvantages* can be theft or loss due to group mismanagement of the funds; depending on where the funds are kept, they might not have federal deposit insurance, group members might not make their deposit when required, and the group might become too large.

Option Five: Savings Bank Account

The *advantages* here are that deposits in federally insured financial institutions are insured up to $250,000 by the FDIC for banks or the NCUA for credit unions. You also may be able to directly deposit wages into your account. You may also be able to automatically move money from checking to savings. You may earn interest. Money is easy to access. It is also a good way to establish a banking relationship.

The *downside* here is the monthly recurring fees that can vary. It is not always the best option for saving money for long-term goals because the interest you earn might be lower than other options. Your financial institution may not be available or you may not have access to online banking or want to use it. You also may have a limited number of withdrawals.

Other Options: There are other even more interesting savings options available today. Contact your financial institution to inquire about their money market deposit accounts, certificates of deposits (CD), US savings bonds, retirement accounts either from your employer or individual retirement accounts (IRA), investments such as stocks, corporate bonds, treasuries, and mutual funds.

5.3 Important Savings Features

Interest Compounding

It is very crucial and important to take advantage of interest compounding where it is available. Interest is simply the money financial institutions pay you for keeping money deposited with them. *Compounding* is earning interest on the interest. Over the long haul, the compounding feature does wonders and makes a significant difference.

Annual Percentage Yield (APY)

The annual percentage yield:

- reflects amount of interest on a yearly basis

- is different from the interest rate

- includes the effect of compounding

- compounds, and the more it does, the higher the APY, and the more interest you earn

- should be used when comparing, as opposed to interest rates

The Rule of 72

This is a formula that estimates how long it will take for money to double, considering a fixed interest rate. Divide 72 by the annual interest rate. The results are the estimated number of years it will take to double the money, assuming:

- no change in interest rate

- no deposits or withdrawals

For example:

On 2% annual interest, it would take 36 years for the money to double. (72/2 = 36)

For an interest rate of 10%, it would take about 7.2 years for the money to double. (72/10 = 7.2)

You can also use the **Rule of 72** to calculate the interest rate required to double the money, given the fixed number of years.

Example: It would require a 12% interest rate per year for the money to double in 6 years. (72/6 = 12)

5.4 Savings For Emergency Expenses

An emergency fund is part of the foundation of a strong financial position. You should strive to maintain at least six (6) months' worth of your monthly expenses aside in your emergency fund.

- It is important to do so because the unexpected happens and events occur no matter how we try to be cautious; we are not capable of accurately anticipating the future.

- If you pay for unexpected expenses with the money you have saved, you avoid creating debt.

- It takes time and commitment.

- It is a cycle.

- Six months is the general rule of thumb because on average and in a healthy job market, even if you lose a job and are actively looking for a new job, you should be able to get one within six months.

5.5 Savings For Your Goals

This is where you save for your hopes and dreams whether they are within a short or intermediate time horizon or for the long term. You save for what you want to have in life, for the future of your family.

As we have seen, your goals must be specific, measurable, action-oriented, reachable, and time-bound. How much money to save depends on

- what you are saving for

- how much it costs

- the time frame you gave yourself to achieve it

Take the money needed, divide it by the time to save, then you see what you need to save at the frequency of your choice (weekly, monthly, quarterly, etc.)

It is important to create a written plan to save money and to stick to the plan.

5.6 Public Benefits

If you are a recipient of public benefits, always bear in mind that some public benefits may be reduced or removed when you exceed income or assets limits. However, some special accounts allow people to save more money without losing *eligibility* for their benefits.

There are assets and income limits to qualify for public benefits in the USA.

- Temporary Assistance for Needy Family (TANF): the limits as of 2023 were $1,000 to 3,000 in most states.

- Supplemental Nutrition Assistance Program (SNAP): it varies by state.

- Medicaid: limits are $2,000 if single, and $3,000 if married, for some disability-linked benefits.

- Supplemental Security Income (SSI): limits are $2,000 if single and $3,000 if married.

- Social Security Disability Income (SSDI): no limits.

ABLE Accounts

There also exists Attainable Saving Plan (ABLE) accounts. The following are some of the characteristics of ABLE Accounts you should familiarize yourself with.

- ABLE accounts offer tax-advantaged savings accounts for individuals with disabilities.

- ABLE accounts are available for the blind or those with other qualifying disabilities that began before their 26th birthday; can be any age when the account is opened.

- You can save money in ABLE accounts without losing eligibility for SSI, Medicaid, or other federal means-tested public benefits.

- You can only have one ABLE account

- There are total annual contribution limits set each year. However, there is a Federal gift tax exclusion limit, which can be higher if account owners contribute earned income, and can include transfers from 529 Accounts.

ABLE accounts also have balance limits; otherwise, eligibility for your current public benefits may be affected. For example:

Up to $100,000: SSI cash benefits continue.

Over $100,000: SSI eligibility is retained but cash benefit is suspended.

Total account limits are set by the sponsoring state. Use the money in your ABLE account for qualified disability expenses. If used for anything else, withdrawal becomes taxable.

Qualified Disability Expenses

The following are qualified disability expenses that you can use your ABLE funds for without incurring or creating a tax event:

- education, housing, transportation

- employment training and support

- assistive technology, personal, and support services

- health care expenses

- financial management and administrative services

- other expenses that help improve health, independence, and/or quality of life

Special Needs Trusts

By definition, special needs trusts are legal arrangements that provide financial security and access to additional funds to someone who is physically or mentally disabled, or chronically ill. They allow for the additional financial support of an individual without potentially affecting other public benefits provided by public assistance programs.

They are designed to fund the long-term expenses and needs of someone with a disability. They can be complicated to set up, so you may need to hire the services of an attorney.

Pooled Special Need Trusts

They provide the benefits of a special needs trust but cost less. A single entity manages many sub-accounts. The trust is usually managed by a non-profit corporation.

Matched Savings Accounts

They encourage saving money for specific purposes, and they are usually run by local community-based organizations. The savings in these accounts are matched by the organizations running programs.

Matched savings accounts have a number of purposes such as job training, college education, small business startup, and purchasing a first home, among others.

It is important to review your financial goals to see if any of these options are the right choices for you to consider as you continue your journey to achieving your financial goals.

6: CREDIT REPORTS AND SCORES

Your credit history can affect your access to credit, loans, some jobs, housing, insurance, and other services. It is important to understand how your credit behavior and bill payment records affect the score and to make sure that you protect your credit history.

6.1 Credit Report

When you receive your credit report, it is important to check for inaccuracies. The following information is reflected in your report, and therefore you should make sure it is accurately reflected.

- your name

- age

- your credit card and other debt payments

- your income

- any bankruptcy records

- cell phone plan payments, if reported

- your student loans payments

- credit cards limits, and other pertinent information

Categories in a Credit Report

The following key categories are listed in your credit report:

- your identifying information

- your debt and bills

- any public records such as bankruptcies

- your application for a new credit card and other hard inquiries

There are three major nationwide credit reporting agencies in the USA. These are **Equifax, Experian**, and **TransUnion**.

A *credit score* is a number based on aggregate information reflected in your credit report.

- It predicts your ability and creditworthiness to pay bills and debt as agreed.

- People with higher credit scores are likely to present a lower risk of default to creditors. The credit score ranges between 300 and 850.

It is important to understand that your credit score is used by several institutions in deciding whether or not a credit or a service can be extended to you. The following are examples of institutions that use credit reports and scores to make decisions about consumers:

- financial institutions, which choose whether or not to accept credit applications such as credit cards, mortgages, lines of credit, et cetera

- some landlords, who choose whether to accept or decline a new tenant, especially in a very competitive housing market

- insurance companies, which in some states, choose to approve or deny an insurance policy

- employers in some states and for some positions, who require good credit as a stipulation to employment

- utilities companies, who may check your credit score before granting a new subscription

Risk-based Pricing

Credit reports and scores may be used as one factor in risk-based pricing. In this case, lenders set interest rates and other terms based on estimated risks.

By law, lenders are required to tell you if and when they used your credit reports or scores to deny your application or offer you less favorable terms. These are known as

- adverse action notices

- risk-based pricing notices

When your credit is invisible or doesn't exist, and you have no credit report, you may have a harder time getting credit or a loan, renting an apartment, getting a favorable cell phone plan, obtaining some jobs, turning on utilities without paying a large deposit, et cetera.

Once again it is important to bear in mind that anyone who uses a credit report to deny your application or offers you less favorable terms for credit, insurance, or employment must tell you they did so. They must give you the contact information for the credit reporting agency they used.

You have the right to know what is in each of your credit reports. You will be required to prove you are who you say you are when you request to see your report.

Opting Out

- You can opt out of receiving prescreened credit offers or insurance, for five years or even permanently.

- You may still get offers based on lists from other sources.

- If you opt out, you can opt back in.

- But you cannot opt out of having a credit report.

6.2 Credit Scores

There are several steps to improving and managing your credit scores. This includes paying your bills on time and as agreed. The basics of credit scoring include the following key elements:

- Your credit score number is calculated from information in credit reports.

- Generally, the higher the number, the better the credit history.

- Your credit score predicts the likelihood of payment of credit obligations on time as agreed.

There are several factors that go into the calculation of your credit score. However, some significant factors affect your credit score more considerably than others. These are:

- **Payment History:** This contains details on whether or not you repay debt on time as agreed, and for how long.

- **Credit Utilization Rate:** This shows the ratio between your approved credit line and the outstanding used balance, meaning what percentage of your credit line you carry each pay period as unpaid balance.

- **Derogatory Marks:** This factor is very consequential and takes a long time to be cleared if incurred. These are marks of major credit events such as bankruptcies, collections, and credit charge-offs, to name a few.

Credit Scoring Metrics

It is possible to have more than one credit score because there are multiple *credit scoring metrics.* The two most prominent and mainstream are

- FICO: Fair Isaac Corporation

- Vantage Score

There are also different models for different types of credit. There are five (5) factors in the General FICO model:

- **New Credit**—10% of your score.

- **Credit Mix** (cards, mortgages, car loans)–this also accounts for 10% of your score.

- **Length of credit history**—how long you have maintained your credit–this accounts for 15% of your score

- **Amount owed**—30% of your score

- **Payment history**— paying on time–this accounts for 35% of your score

Make sure that your credit score accurately reflects the information in your credit report. Regularly, get and review your credit report and dispute errors.

Credit Rating

Based on FICO, scores are rated in the following manner:

800-850: Exceptional/Excellent

740 - 799: Very good

670 - 739: Good (majority of people are in this range)

580 - 669: Fair

300 - 579: Poor

6.3 Know Your Rights And Watch Out

You have the right to free credit reports; at least one free credit report every 12 months from each nationwide credit reporting agency: Equifax, Experian, and TransUnion. Go to www.annualcreditreport.com and fill out orders for these free credit reports.

Watch out for imposters:

- These are companies that advertise free credit reports, credit scores, or credit monitoring services but are not part of the legally mandated free annual credit report program.

- Sometimes, the free services convert to ones you have to pay for after the trial period.

Simply go to the website provided above, and complete the online form with your name, date of birth, social security number, current address, and previous addresses if you have lived at your current address for less than two years. Once on the website:

- Pick the report you want: Equifax, Experian, or TransUnion.

- For each of the three reports, you will complete an additional form that includes security questions based on the information from your credit report.

You have the right to additional free credit reports if:

- you receive public assistance

- you are unemployed and looking for a job

- you are a victim of identity theft or financial fraud

- you have been denied credit, service, an apartment, or employment based on your credit history

Should you need more credit scores beyond the free legally mandated ones, you can contact:

- some of the nonprofit organizations

- credit card companies through statements or websites

- FICO www.myfico.com

- VantageScore www.vantagescore.com

6.4 Dispute Errors

There are a number of possible errors which can be reflected on your credit reports and affect the overall score if not detected and corrected in a timely manner. Some of the errors to watch for are:

- identity errors

- incorrect reporting of account status

- data management errors

- balance errors

- outdated information

There is a time limit on negative information such as debt collections records that may be reported on your credit report. This is generally seven years. However, some bankruptcies are an exception.

Note that there is no time limit for negative information when someone applies for:

- a job with a yearly salary of $75,000 or more

- more than $150,000 worth of credit

- life insurance with a face value of $150,000 or more

The 7-year reporting period can be confusing. It generally starts 180 days after you stop paying on the debt.

Medical debts are generally not on credit reports until unpaid for at least 180 days. This grace period:

- provides time to resolve medical billing disputes

- allows you to make payments or make arrangements if you cannot pay in full

When you dispute an error in your credit report, make sure you provide your complete name and mailing address, a clear description of each item you are disputing, and the reason for each dispute. Then you may request for correction or removal.

You may need to provide supporting information such as sending copies of your material elements in dispute– receipts, credit card account statements, images of checks, or screenshots of online transactions or automatic bill payments.

After you file a dispute, the credit agency will send you a letter. If there is agreement on incorrect information, that information cannot be put back on your report again. Check your new report to make sure incorrect information has been removed. You can also request notices of corrections to be sent to individuals or businesses that received your initial incorrect report.

6.5 Build, Repair, And Improve Credit History

As widely discussed earlier, the very first key pointers to getting your credit report in order are:

- Get and review your credit reports.

- Dispute and correct errors.

- Pay all of your bills on time as agreed.

- Use as little of your credit limit as possible.

- Use a credit-building strategy.

- Keep old accounts open if you can.

- Apply for credit only if you need it.

- Negotiate better terms.

- Ask for a **goodwill deletion.** This is an extremely effective way to have a creditor who has reported negative information, reconsider and remove the information from your report, especially if you have had a major life event that genuinely prevented you from being able to pay your bills on time.

Repairing a bad credit history does take a long time to yield substantial results and therefore build an alternative credit history that can help you get some services in the meantime.

Document other payments and obligations you regularly make on time as proof of your creditworthiness. For example, rent payments, child care, cell phone bills, electric bills, gas bills, TV, service bills, internet bills, insurance payments, loans from family or friends, and savings.

Building a good credit report also takes a number of steps depending on whether you are building from scratch or want to better your existing history:

- Get a secured credit card.

- Get a credit-building loan.

- Become an authorized user on an account.

- Apply for a credit card at a store or gas station.

- Make a large down payment, and negotiate a loan from the balance.

Get help. There is no shame in seeking help when you need it.

- Contact your financial institution to see if they have a credit counseling desk available to their customers.

- There are a few nonprofit consumer credit counseling services; take advantage of that.

- Reach out to the housing counseling agency, approved by the Department of Housing and Urban Planning.

- Find Volunteer and Pro Bono certified financial planners to help.

There are credit repair companies that promise to fix your credit for a fee.

Debt consolidation businesses also offer different services and often specialize in debt consolidation loans and debt settlement services. Be cautious and understand all available options to make sure they are right for you or walk away. Debt consolidation is simply taking out a new loan to pay off other debts and does not address underlying causes of debt.

Debt settlement is a way of working with creditors to accept a lower payment and settle debt. You may have to pay income tax on the portion that was settled.

Beware of credit repair scams. There are the people who:

- promise to erase bad credit or remove other negative, but accurate, information

- promise fast and easy credit repair

- offer to create a new identity for you

- want you to pay their service fee upfront

- will not tell you about your rights

It is important to protect your **credit history** and **credit fraud** by being aware of the following:

- initial fraud alert

- active duty military alert

- extended fraud alert

- credit freeze

- credit lock

7: BORROWING FUNDAMENTALS

7.1 Borrowing Options and Costs

When borrowing, I cannot stress enough the importance of making sure you can afford the payments before getting a loan. Also, know how much it will cost and what will happen if you cannot pay the loan back.

Borrowing simply means that the lender provides you with money and you must pay it back with interest, most of the time.

Credit is defined as one's ability to borrow money, how much, and on what terms, while **debt** simply means you owe to a person or business.

Types of Loans

There are a few types of loans to consider when borrowing or financing any purchase.

1. **Installment loans** are usually repaid in equal payments over a set period of time. Examples include most fixed-rate mortgages, auto loans, and student loans.

2. **Revolving loans** are repaid based on how much you have borrowed. Examples include most credit cards and home equity lines of credit.

Other Financing Options

Rent-to-own services: These are not loans per se, but they can provide you with other other flexible options if getting a loan is not an option.

It is important to know that:

- this is not a loan

- you can buy an item for a period of time and make monthly or weekly rental payments

- rental payments are partly credited toward the purchase price

- the store can take back the item if you miss a payment or wish to cancel agreements

Please note that the longer time making payments, the more you end up paying for the item.

Buying on Layaway

This is yet another option to acquire an item without necessarily applying for a traditional loan. It has some similarities with the Rent-To-Own option but you cannot take the item until it has been paid for. This is how it works:

- It is not a loan.

- You make an initial deposit for an item, then make payment for the balance over time.

- The store holds merchandise until paid in full.

- Layaway plans may include fees, consequences of late or missed payments, et cetera. Make sure you understand the terms and refund policy.

Natures of Loans

When it comes to credit and loan approval criteria and requirements, there are typically two natures of loans:

1. **Secured loans:** They require collateral such as your house, your vehicle, or cash. Bear in mind that you lose the collateral to the lender if you don't pay as agreed.

2. **Unsecured loans:** They have no collateral. They often have higher interest rates than secured loans because of the lack of guarantees. The credit is approved based on the borrower's creditworthiness.

The Cost of Borrowing

The convenience of accessing funds through borrowing comes with the fact that:

- you generally repay more than you borrowed

- principal is the amount of money you borrowed

- interest is the amount of money a financial institution charges for allowing you to use its money

- fees may be charged for certain activities such as reviewing loan applications

Prepayment

There are two types of prepayment:

- an early repayment of all of a loan, which essentially reduces interest cost and pays off the loan.

- an early payment of PART of a loan, which generally reduces interest costs and potentially permits an earlier payoff date.

Some loans have prepayment penalties, others do not.

The Truth In Lending Act (TILA) requires lenders to make written loan disclosures to borrowers. Borrowers must:

- be shown loan terms in a clear and uniform manner

- receive the TILA disclosure before the customer signs

The TILA requirement is very customer-friendly because it allows you to compare loan offers.

TILA Disclosure must show the following elements:

- Annual Percentage Rate (APR): This is the cost of your credit as a yearly rate. For example: 5% APR.

- Finance Charge: This is the dollar amount the credit will cost you. Example: $500

- Amount Financed: This is the amount of credit provided to you on your behalf. For example: $10,000.

- Total of Payments: This is the amount you will have paid after you have made all payments as scheduled. For example: $10,500.

TILA disclosures are also applicable to mortgages (home loans) and some student loans.

It is recommended that you shop around by using TILA disclosures, particularly the annual percentage rates (APR) to compare offers. If needed, seek help.

- There are housing counseling agencies approved by the U.S. Department of Housing and Urban Development.

- There are credit counseling organizations.

7.2 Loan Application Process

As you prepare for a loan application, knowing what lenders look for when deciding to loan money is essential. Methods vary by lender. Some of the factors lenders may use to make decisions on a loan application include the following but are not limited to

- your credit, also known as character

- your capacity

- your capital

- your collateral (for secured loans only)

- conditions

Credit (Character)

This is an indicator of how you have paid your bills or your debt. Your credit report and scores are used to evaluate:

- how you have used credit in the past

- how many credit accounts you have

- if you have ever filed for bankruptcy

- If you've had property repossessed or foreclosed on

- if you've made late payments, etc

Capacity

This is your present and future ability to meet your payments. Lenders will assess:

- how much of your income goes to pay debt

- your debt-to-income ratio

- how long you have been employed

- how much you make each month

- what your monthly expenses are.

Capital

This is the value of your current assets and net-worth. Lender are interested to see:

- how much money is in your checking and savings accounts.

- the value of your investment and other assets.

- your total net-worth.

Net Worth = Total Assets - Total Liabilities

Collateral

This is for secured loans only. There are the assets that will secure the loan. For example, your house or land are common collaterals.

Conditions

This depends on the type of loan.

Co-borrowing And Cosigning Loans

Co-borrowing is simply taking out a loan jointly with others. You must pay the debt even if your co-borrowers do not. With cosigning, however, the loan proceeds go to the borrower, not the cosigner. The cosigner promises to pay the debt if the borrower does not.

Before cosigning the loan, always ask yourself the following questions:

- Can I afford the loan alone? Consider the worst-case scenario. If the borrower does not make payments, and you have to make them, and possibly also pay late fees and collection fees, can you afford it?

- Will cosigning the loan affect my ability to get other loans I might need in the foreseeable future?

When you cosign, the debt appears on your credit report until fully paid by the borrower. If this debt is ever in default, that fact might become part of your credit history, even after it's been paid off, which would affect your credit scores.

Also, if you want to get other credit, lenders might consider the cosigned loan as one of your debts when they are determining your capacity to take on new debts.

Remember, before you apply for credit, co-borrow, or cosign, ask and assess yourself through the lenses of a lender, to see if you have a fair shot at being approved.

- Is your capacity, capital, credit, or collateral going to reflect on you positively or negatively?

- If any of these are not in good shape, what can you do to improve them before you head to the lender for a loan application?

7.3 Borrowing When Someone Else Manages Your Money

During some of life's stages or circumstances such as infirmity or old age, we sometimes appoint someone else to help us manage our money and make some of the non-material decisions for us. With this responsibility, you need to make sure they are:

- acting in your best interest, when they have fiduciary responsibility for you

- managing your money and property carefully

- keeping your money and property separate from theirs

- keeping good records

- including you in decision-making to the extent possible

What to discuss:

- You should ask the person managing your money why you need to borrow.

- Do you have enough resources to repay the loan?

- How will you make payments on the loan?

- Will it affect any of your other sources of income such as public benefits?

- What is the best borrowing option for your needs?

If you decide to borrow money:

- You can get help considering the terms.

- You can get help completing the application.

- The lender will decide if you are a good credit risk.

- Lender will not consider the creditworthiness of the person helping you.

- Ask for help if you need reminding to make timely payments and keep good records.

8: DEBT MANAGEMENT

8.1 Understanding Debt

Understanding debt is the first step to managing it. It is also equally important to know the difference between credit and debt. Debt is the actual money you owe; while credit is your ability to borrow money as new debt or to restructure the existing one. You use credit to borrow money, which then becomes your debt, once borrowed.

The difference between **debtor** and **creditor** is that debtors owe money to creditors or lenders.

- Debtors owe money (they borrowed it).

- Creditors and lenders loan money to debtors.

In order to fully understand your debt, you need to know the following key elements:

- Who do you owe money to?

- How much do you owe them?

- How much are the payments?

- When are the payments due?

- Other important facts about your debt such as prepayment penalties, fixed or flexible interest rates, promotional rates if any, default consequences, etc.

There are a number of reasons why people get into debt, including but not limited to:

- needing to pay bills, or sometimes as a result of not paying them

- covering unexpected expenses or emergencies

- purchasing items they want or need

- financing projects for investments

Understanding how debt acquisition can affect your overall financial situation is crucial to maintaining financial security. Below are some of the impacts of taking on debt:

- There might be a need to use your future income to service your current debt, also known as *"obligating future income."*

- You generally pay interest and sometimes fees on your debt, until paid.

- Your current debt may impact how soon you can achieve your goals, by either getting you there faster or slowing you down.

8.2 How Debt Functions

In order to make informed decisions about debt, you must understand how debt works:

- First of all, understand that *secured* loans are debt with collateral, which means a lender can put a lien on a property and take it if the loan is not paid according to the loan agreement.

- *Principal* is how much money you borrow.

- *Interest* is the main cost of borrowing.

- *Revolving* credit is a credit agreement that allows you to borrow money from time to time up to a pre-approved maximum credit line.

- The *Annual Percentage Rate (APR)* is the total cost of credit on a yearly basis.

- An *installment* loan is when you borrow a specific amount of money and repay it over a set period of time.

- An *unsecured* loan is a loan with no collateral, where a lender loans you money purely based on your creditworthiness.

- The *term* of a loan is how long you have to repay the principal and interest.

For **installment** loans, you generally pay the same amount every payment unless there is a variable or adjustable interest rate that affects the amount of payment.

For **revolving** credit, the credit limit is the maximum amount of money you can borrow.

- Payment is based on credit you have used.

- Minimum payments are often 1% to 5% of the outstanding balance.

- Paying more toward the debt means the debt will be paid off sooner, and therefore you will save on interest.

Fees: There are additional charges besides interest. It is important to understand the fees you may be charged, depending on the circumstances or use of the credit.

Prepayment is simply the early payment of all or part of a loan. It reduces interest costs; it may also mean an earlier payoff date.

Some loans will charge a prepayment penalty if paid too early. Inquire with your lender about any possible prepayment fees before commitment.

8.3 Debt Reduction

It takes a solid plan to reduce your debt or, ideally, eliminate it. Get help from a trained credit counselor or a financial advisor if needed. There is more than one method of reducing debt. The most common methods include but are not limited to the following:

The *High-Cost Debt First Method* has the advantage of saving money, but progress may feel slower:

- List your debts from the highest cost to you to the lowest.

- Pay the amount due on each debt.

- Make extra payments to the first debt on the list.

- After you pay off the first debt, make extra payments on the next debt on the list.

- Continue as needed.

The *Snowball Method:* The advantage here is that it makes progress seem faster. The disadvantage is that you may pay more money.

- List your debts, from lowest balance to highest.

- Pay the amount due on each debt.

- Make extra payments to the first debt on the list.

- After you pay off the first debt, make extra payment on the next debt on the list

- Continue as needed

Get help

If needed, reach out to the following for assistance:

- Nonprofit credit counseling organizations.

- The Federal Trade Commission (FTC). They can give you tips on how to find and choose a credit counselor.

- You can also go to www.usa.gov and search for Credit Counseling.

Choose Help Carefully

Debt *Settlement* companies offer to make deals with your creditors. Make sure you ask them about fees and processes.

Debt *Consolidation* loans offer one loan you can use to pay off multiple loans. Make sure you ask them about interest rates, fees, and other costs. Make sure the interest rates they offer are fixed rates for the life of the debt rather than teaser rates.

Always ask more questions if the company you are working with:

- charges fees before it will settle your debts

- guarantees it can make your debt go away

- guarantees that your debt can be paid off for pennies on the dollar

- tells you it can stop all debt collection calls and lawsuits

- tells you not to communicate with your creditors while they negotiate a better deal

8.4 Debt Default And Debt Collection

It is advisable to not ignore a debt collector. Always make sure that any debt you are asked to pay is reconciled as soon as possible. Get help if you need it. You want your debt payment status to remain *current* if you are still making payments.

When you take on debt and make payments on time as agreed, your debt payment status is current.

Debt— > Pay Ontime As Agreed—- > Current

When you take on debt and miss payments or do not pay the amount as agreed; your status becomes *delinquent*; then becomes *charged off* before it gets assigned to internal *collections* or sold to *debt collectors.*

Several things can happen if you don't pay your debts as agreed:

- Late fees or more money in interest can accrue.

- You can be contacted by debt collectors.

- You can lose services or have to pay extra to reestablish them.

- You can lose your collateral.

- You can receive negative entries on your credit reports.

- Your credit score may drop.

- You can receive a lawsuit from creditors.

- You can have your wages garnished.

- You can have your account garnished.

- You can be subject to the Treasury Offset Program.

If you have any debt in collections, make sure that you are paying what you actually owe, and send payments only to someone who can legitimately collect on that debt. Debt collectors can contact you by phone or by mail, therefore make sure you address their inquiries in a timely fashion.

Any debt collector who contacts you claiming you owe payment on a debt is required by law to tell you certain information about the debt:

- They must tell the name of the current creditor if the debt has been sold off, and

- They must inform you of the total amount you owe.

They also must tell you that:

- You can dispute the debt.

- If you don't dispute the debt within 30 days in writing, the debt collector will assume the debt is valid.

Before you make a plan to pay a debt, Be sure that:

- you actually owe the debt.

- the statute of limitation has not expired.

- you are dealing with a legitimate debt collector.

If all these items above are verified, you need to pay the debt in full if possible. If payment in full is not possible:

- Set up a payment plan and make sure it is a plan you can afford to maintain.

- Negotiate a lower balance; always ask for **"paid in full"** and not **"settled."**

Debt collectors must follow rules such as

- no abusive, unfair, or deceptive practices

- no inconvenient times or places

- no calls at work if told not to call

- no threats of violence

- No obscene or profane language.

You should report problems with debt collectors if needed.

8.5 Student Loan Debt

It is very important to consider your options and understand what will happen if you are late with payments when it is time to pay back your student loans. Your student loans servicer can help you explore repayment plans.

Student debt is simply defined as money owed on student loans and is probably the biggest debt some people will ever have in their lifetime. It is sometimes a stressful topic.

There are severe consequences if you don't repay your student loans such as

- paying more in fees and interest

- wage garnishment

- account garnishment

- treasury offset

- inability to get more federal student aid in the future

- negative entries on credit reports

- decrease in credit scores

- decreased ability to borrow money for other use

- delay in reaching other financial goals

There are typically *two types* of student loans:

- Private student loans

- Federal Student loans

In this chapter we will only focus on **federal** student loans. There are several federal student loan repayment options including a

- grace period

- standard repayment plan

- restructured payments NOT based on income, including the Graduated Repayment Plan and the Extended Repayment Plan

There are, however, repayment plans based on income such as:

- Revised Pay As You Earn plan (REPAYE)

- Pay As You Earn plan (PAYE)

- Income-Based Repayment plan (IBR)

- Income-Contingent Repayment plan (ICR)

There are also forbearance and deferment Options:

Forbearance is a temporary postponement or reduction of payments due to financial difficulty.

Deferment is the temporary suspension of loan payments for specific situations.

There are also occasional loan forgiveness, cancellation, and discharges such as:

- Closed School discharge

- Public Service Loan Forgiveness

- Teacher Loan Forgiveness

- Total and Permanent Disability Discharge

- Discharge due to Death

Always make sure you do the best you can and take preemptive action to prevent default. Some of the actions you may take include

- asking for a different payment due date

- asking for a different repayment plan option

- asking for forbearance, deferment, loan forgiveness, loan cancellation, or loan discharge

Note that declaring bankruptcy does not automatically discharge federal student loans.

What To Keep In Mind

There are some student loans scams that

- persuade you to pay an upfront fee

- promise fast loan forgiveness

- have a Department of Education seal, which does not necessarily mean they are legitimate

- want your private information, such as your Federal Student Aid Identification Number (FSA ID)–do not share this number

It is important to always

- know the type of loan you have, which will determine the repayment options available to you

- read your promissory note or loan agreement

- keep good records, including any school financial aid award letters, and loan counseling materials such as entrance counseling and exit counseling

8.6 Medical Debt

Medical debt is the result of not paying all of your medical bills when they are due. You don't start out with debt when you receive medical care. You receive medical care and then get a bill for the care. Any medical bill that is not paid is what becomes a medical debt.

Medical bills often turn into medical debt for a number of reasons, such as the fact that they are often unplanned, total costs are not known upfront, and expenses quickly add up.

They can be confusing because

- multiple individuals may provide separate care with separate billing

- there may be a lack of understandable details

- insurance information is often unknown

What to do when you receive what looks like a medical bill:

- Make sure you are looking at an actual bill.

- Read it carefully. It could be an explanation of benefits, which is not a bill. It is a document that lists the charges for medical products or services received. It shows how much money you are responsible for paying, and what your health insurance, if any, is responsible for paying.

- If it is a bill, review it carefully. Do the dates listed on the bill match the actual dates you received the care?

- If you have insurance, check that your insurance company paid what it was supposed to pay.

- If you do not owe what the bill shows that you owe, dispute it quickly. The bill should indicate who you need to contact for any inquiries, including disputes.

If you truly owe what the bill says you owe, try to pay it in full. If you cannot pay in full, try to negotiate a lower payment amount. If you don't have insurance, ask for the uninsured rate. Ask for a discount. Also, most service providers are willing to work out a one-time settlement offer to pay in full, rather than a long-term payment plan with risks of default.

If full payment is still not possible:

- set up a payment plan and honor it

- settle the debt for less

- work with nonprofit credit counseling organizations

- consider bankruptcy

When it comes to medical debt in collections, unpaid debt appears on credit reports 180 days after the first missed payment. Debt can still be referred to collections. For credit scores, treatment of medical debt varies.

8.7 High-Cost Debt

It is advisable that you understand how high-cost debt works, in order to be able to identify lower-cost options in the future.

High-cost debts are the result of small-dollar, short-term loans with costly fees, or high-interest rates, or both. There are risks and benefits with all financial products and services, including high-cost debt.

Vehicle Title loans are loans for a small amount of money for a short time. These loans take vehicle title as collateral, and they are often single-payment loans due in 30 days. They can be very expensive.

Payday Advance Loans

- The borrower visits a payday lender in person or online to get a new loan, or the borrower reborrows a prior loan.

- The borrower gives the lender a personal check dated 14 to 30 days in the future or gives permission for an automatic withdrawal from an account.

- The lender gives the borrower the amount of the loan.

- When a loan is due, if the borrower doesn't have the money to cover the check or withdrawal, the loan is reborrowed with more fees.

Pawn Shop Loans

With pawn shop loans, the item you pawn is the collateral. The loan amount is usually 25% to 50% of how much a pawn shop considers an item to be worth. You must repay the loan, renew it, or lose the pawned item such as jewelry.

Alternatives to High-Cost Debt

There are a number of alternatives to consider before you take on high-cost debt:

- Think about why you need to borrow money. Do you need a loan in order to pay for a need, an obligation, or a want? If it is a want, consider spending less money for it, not buying it at all, or waiting until you have the money to pay for it.

- Explore options in your community. There may be programs offering assistance in paying bills, such as utility bills, or medical bills.

- Instead of borrowing money as a way to pay a bill, try to negotiate for more time to pay the bill or set up a payment plan.

- Use lower-cost alternatives from financial institutions. They may offer small-dollar credit-building loans. Do not assume that you will not qualify. Find out.

- Use your emergency savings, if any.

- Borrow from a friend or family.

- Consider using a credit card. It will increase your monthly credit card payment, but it could be cheaper in the long run.

In summary, there are **good debts** and **bad debts**. Good debts carry lower interest rates and can help build assets. They also may be tax-deductible. Bad debts, however, usually carry the highest interest rates and can be very costly over time, especially when you borrow to acquire something that loses value rather than being a productive asset.

9: CREDIT CARDS

9.1 Understanding Credit Cards

Knowing how credit works is very important because it helps with effectively shopping around for the card that meets your goals. To understand credit cards, you need to first understand what a credit card is.

- A credit card is simply a revolving line of credit.

- It is a convenient way to buy goods and services by using a credit line extended to you by the creditor.

- It's an opportunity to buy now, pay later.

- There is a limit on how much you can borrow (credit limit or credit line).

- You must pay at least a portion of the bill every billing cycle (minimum payment).

Although some consumers hold a negative view on the usage of credit cards, it is fair to say that credit cards are important financial tools to

- help build evidence that you are creditworthy, which is important to lenders for your future financing needs

- help you pay for emergency expenses in case you do not have enough funds in your emergency fund

- make purchases conveniently online or by phone

Using credit cards as your purchase payment method also allows you to dispute erroneous credit card charges, and to dispute certain charges for goods and services that weren't delivered as agreed.

There are also cards that are usually treated like credit cards although they are essentially not credit cards. These are **charge cards**, prepaid cards also known as stored value cards, as well as debit cards.

The **Truth in Lending Disclosure Act** states that lenders must show you all relevant written disclosures, which contain important information such as rates and fees. This is necessary because credit card rates and fees vary greatly.

Interest Rates

There are several types of rates and fees on credit cards:

- Annual Percentage Rate (APR): this is a cost of credit expressed as a yearly rate.

- Penalty AP: this is the amount of increased rate if you don't pay the bill on time.

- Interest rates: they can be fixed or variable.

Low introductory APRs are *teaser rates*, which last for a limited time, normally six months to a year, then go back up to normal rates. For example, you may get a 0% interest on purchases for 18 months, then a variable APR of 14.99% to 29.99% moving forward.

When using the card, bear in mind those low introductory rates and subsequent variable rates. Try to pay off the card balance during the introductory period to take advantage of low to no fees.

Credit card *rewards* are additional perks given to certain users. The type of rewards and the amount received depend on the credit card rewards calculation metrics. Some examples of rewards include but are not limited to

- rebates

- points

- airline travel miles

- cashback

It is very important to

- know how to qualify

- understand how to maintain rewards because some rewards must be redeemed during a certain period before expiration

- make sure rewards do not induce/cause you to overspend

- consider fees when you look at rewards and decide if extra rewards make up for extra fees you might be charged

- shop around. All rewards are not created equal

Credit Limit

This is the maximum credit you can use on the card. Each creditor has its own standards to set the credit limit, but they all typically consider your credit history, current income, and outstanding debt, to name a few.

The **Grace period** is the time between when your statement is issued and when your payment is due. Creditors do not have to give grace periods but most creditors do anyway. It is usually 14 to 21 days.

The *Balance Computation Method* shows how interest on your account is calculated. There are different methods, and cardholder agreements will include which method is used. One of the most common methods is the *"Average Daily Balance Method."*

Pay attention to your card agreement and ask your financial institution or card issuer if you have any questions regarding how interest on your balance will be calculated.

Credit cards have other features, products, and services that are important to know:

- customer service features

- extended warranty feature for free

- payment protection and credit monitoring, among others

Secured credit cards:

- are for using money you already have (collateral) in a dedicated deposit account, and the balance is equal to the card's credit limit.

- can improve your credit history and scores if you pay the balance regularly by the due date..

- are usually easier to qualify for than unsecured cards.

- help repair, and rebuild credit history.

- typically have a lower credit limit.

Application for a credit card is a straightforward process. Financial institutions and retail stores offer ways to apply for credit cards. There are also comparison websites that help you shop around. On some occasions, you may also receive pre-approved offers in the mail.

It is important to understand the key terms in the credit card application process such as the credit card applicant, creditor, individual credit, joint credit, authorized user, et cetera.

9.2 Credit Card Management

Credit cards can be very convenient. However, it is very important to manage them carefully to keep costs down and avoid damage to your credit. Therefore, being able to read and understand your credit card statement is very crucial.

- Account billing cycle is the time period covered by the statement.

- Account summary shows the new balance, credit limit, and credit available.

- Payment information shows the minimum payment due, payment due date, late payment warning, and total minimum payment warning.

- There is also a credit counseling statement printed.

- You would receive a notice of interest rate charges, if any.

- You will see account activities including transactions, finance charges, annual fee, and interest totals.

- You will see your interest charge calculation.

These are some of the important steps to managing your credit card:

- Keep good records.

- Check statements for mistakes.

- Understand the impacts of different payment strategies.

- Try to keep the credit balance (what you owe) very low compared to the credit limit.

Practical Examples

Paying only the monthly minimum payment, as tempting as it sounds, can hurt you in the long run. For example, an item that costs $500 on a credit card with 18% APR, would end up costing $132 in interest paid; which means the item will cost a total of $632. It would take three years to pay it off.

For an item that costs $2,500 at 18% APR, it would result in $5,363 in interest paid. The total cost of the item would be $7,863 and it would take 23 years to pay it off. However, the same $2,500 item, at 18% APR would only cost $3.254 total ($754 interest paid) and would only be paid off in 3 years if you pay the monthly minimum plus an extra $41 dollars per month. For $24 per month extra, the same item would take about 4 years, and would cost $3,525 total ($1,025 interest). Note that all figures in these examples are rounded to the nearest dollar.

The way payments are applied to your balance is also something important to understand. For minimum payment only, creditors choose how to apply to balance, and they often apply that balance to portions of the balance with the lowest interest rate. When you pay an extra amount over the minimum, it is generally applied to the portion of the balance with the highest interest rate.

Summary *tips to manage* your credit card effectively include the following:

- Review your statement as soon as you receive it. Contact the creditor right away if you notice errors, such as charges for an item you did not purchase.

- Pay off your balance in full each month to save money and avoid paying interest. If you can't do that, pay as much as you can, as soon as you can.

- Pay on time. Avoid late fees and late payment records on your credit report. If you cannot pay, call the creditor right away. The creditor may waive late fees or be willing to make other payment arrangements.

- Try to minimize how much you owe in relation to your credit limit. This is your *credit utilization rate*. Some experts advise using no more than *30%* of your credit limit while others advise using no more than *20%*. While keeping balances at or below those percentages may not always be realistic, it helps to use as little of your credit limit as possible.

- Know that using a high percentage of your credit limit at any point in the billing cycle can negatively affect your credit scores. This is true even if you regularly pay off the entire balance every month.

- Keep a record of important information about your credit cards. This includes keeping your account numbers and expiration dates, among others, private

to avoid being a victim of fraud or identity theft.

10: BUILDING A FINANCIAL FOUNDATION

10.1 Understanding Assets

Understanding the meaning of assets and how to accumulate them is very important because asset accumulation can lead to wealth and financial security. An **asset** is something you own that has value. There are two main types of assets to consider:

- **physical** assets also known as **tangible assets** such as land, machinery, vehicles, equipment, tools, or gold

- **financial** assets known as **intangible assets** such as stocks, bonds, funds held in a bank, investments, accounts receivable, company goodwill, copyrights, patents, et cetera

The main similarity between physical and financial assets is that they both represent an economic resource that can be converted into value, and both assets are recorded in a firm's balance sheet.

Here are the main differences:

- Physical assets are tangible and financial assets are not.

- Physical assets usually depreciate or lose value due to wear and tear, whereas financial assets do not experience such a reduction in value due to depreciation.

- Financial assets may lose value due to changes in market interest rates, a fall in investment returns, or a fall in the stock market prices.

- Physical assets also require maintenance, upgrades, and repairs, whereas financial assets do not incur such expenses.

The value of your assets is determined based on the type of assets. There are key benefits of asset building such as

- financial security because they generate income

- providing a foundation for your financial future

- achieving long-term financial stability and growing wealth

Owning a diverse range of assets:

- allows you to create a "buffer" to handle emergencies

- helps you reach your goals

- increases your options

- helps you earn more income

- inspires you to look to the future

- reduces stress and increases the quality of life.

10.2 Assets As A Financial Foundation

Your net worth is a good measure of your financial stability.
Calculate your net worth by subtracting your total liabilities
(money you owe others) from your total assets. **Equity** is
defined as the value of an asset minus the liability related to
that asset.

Equity = Value of Asset - Related Liability

For example, home equity is the difference between the market value of a home and the money owed on the mortgage, if any.

Your net worth is the measure of your financial wealth. It equals your personal total assets minus your total liabilities. Or the total equity from all of your assets added together.

Net Worth = Assets - Liability

A positive net worth means a financial cushion. Zero or negative net worth means no financial cushion and can essentially translate into financial instability.

To calculate your net worth:

- The first step is to list all your assets and add them together to reach the total value of your assets.

- The second step is to list all liabilities and calculate total liabilities.

- Finally, calculate total assets minus total liabilities.

In order to change your net worth, you can either increase your assets, decrease your liability, or do both. There are a number of specific ways people can increase their net worth such as:

- spending less than you make

- buying less than you can afford

- saving money

- using employer programs

- using debt responsibly

- paying down your debt

- exploring public benefits

- claiming tax credits

- shopping around

- building more assets

10.3 Cars as Assets

A car can be a productive asset when it helps you get other assets. Plan ahead to get a car you can afford with as little debt as possible. Cars can be productive assets in a way that:

- Safe and reliable transportation is part of financial security.

- A car increases your choice of jobs or access to medical services, education, child care, or elder care.

However, does owning a car always make you better off financially? It depends on whether it is a productive car; which means, if the car helps you earn more money than spent on maintenance. Also, it depends on whether you fully pay for it in cash or have to take debt on it with interest.

It is very important to make sure that you buy a car that you can afford. Now the question is, how much car can you afford? There is no precise formula to decide. But there are a few elements to consider. Some guidelines and questions can help.

- Start with your spending and saving plan to see how the new purchase is going to affect your existing plan.

- Remember to include the cost of insurance, maintenance and repairs, gas/other fuel, title, and registration, to name a few.

10.4 Training and Education as Assets

Training and education can be productive assets when they give you a strong chance at securing a better career or higher-paying job. Plan ahead to pay for them with as little debt as possible.

- They can lead to higher wages.

- They can be an important part of your asset-building strategy.

- They can be smart investments toward meeting goals.

- They may be paths to higher pay and great careers.

There are several types of educational experiences and institutions such as:

- on-the-job training

- apprenticeships

- vocational or career and technical schools

- community colleges

- four-year colleges

- military

- Job Corps, AmeriCorps, and the Peace Corps

In order to pursue education and training, you may need to invest your own resources such as time and money. You also may need to take on student loans.

Think of opportunity cost to make sure that the time spent in school is worthwhile because time spent in school may be time not spent earning money.

Do your research to see if training and education is a smart investment for you:

- Keep in mind the school, training program, record of job placement, cost, and related items.

- This doesn't mean you shouldn't pursue training or education–find the one that fits your needs and budget.

- Make an informed decision.

Ask yourself questions such as what is the future earnings potential, job security, and market demand of the career or job you are planning to pursue. Also, bear in mind the cost of the school program or training you are planning to attend. Will you be able to pay bills and keep a positive cash flow?

Should you elect to pursue further education or training as a means to build your financial future, there are a number of ways to pay for it:

- Ask for help from friends and family.

- Save money now or use saved money.

- Work while attending school.

- Apply for scholarships and grants.

- Ask for help from your employer.

- Borrow money using student loans.

- Or a combination of the above.

Most scholarships are merit-based which means they are awarded to students with certain qualifications such as academic or athletic ability. They are also usually very competitive. Grants, however, are mostly need-based. They are usually awarded based on your financial situation, and they may also be competitive.

As part of building your financial future through furthering your education or training, there are a few ways to save money for it such as:

- **529 Plans**: These plans help save money for future education costs. They are usually tax deductible. Rules vary by state.

- **ABLE Accounts (529A Plans)**: This is for individuals of any age with significant disabilities that began before their 26th birthday. They can use funds for education.

In case you have to take out some student loans to fund your education, consider both federal and private loans. Also, you don't have to borrow the maximum amount offered to you. Only borrow what you need.

It would be wise to maintain your total student debt below your projected starting annual salary.

Total Student Debt < Starting Annual Salary

Federal student loans are offered by the federal government.

- They usually have lower interest rates and offer better repayment terms, benefits, and options than private student loans.

- Repayment generally starts after a student leaves school.

It is important to pay back the student loans on time. Also, note that student loans are not automatically discharged by bankruptcy.

- Non-payment can possibly result in referral to a debt collection agency, drop in credit scores, wage garnishment, et cetera.

- Non-payment also means the loan amount can keep growing due to compounded interest, which increases your total liabilities, therefore negatively affecting your net-worth.

10.5 Investment And Retirement Assets

In better economic times, there are options that offer both safety and steady growth for your money, in order to not only help you preserve your assets but also to accumulate even more assets.

Some of the most popular 'save-and-grow your investable assets' are the following:

1. **Money market accounts**: They typically offer a higher annual percentage yield (APY) than a conventional savings account; though they also generally require a higher minimum balance. Money in this type of account is also generally easy to access.

2. **Certificates of Deposits (CDs)**: CDs are "**time-deposits**". Each has a specific time range (typically from one month up to ten years) and usually a higher fixed interest rate. The money placed in CDs matures until the specific time range is over. Penalty fees are typically charged for cashing in a CD before its maturity date. You will lose interest if you take the money out before the money has matured. Therefore, these vehicles are best for money you don't plan to access for a while.

3. **Individual Retirement Accounts (IRA)**: A traditional IRA (as well as a Roth IRA and other retirement accounts) is another method of saving that typically has certain tax advantages.

4. **Investment Accounts:** Investment accounts also known as brokerage accounts typically involve investing in vehicles like stocks and bonds, which

have the highest potential for growth but also can carry substantial risk. Any investment in the stock or bond market—including mutual funds— is subject to market volatility that can cause an investment to drop (or gain) value unpredictably.

US Savings Bond: This is a saving product issued and guaranteed by the U.S. government. The most common types are Series EE and Series I savings bonds. Savings bonds are lower-risk options than stocks or mutual funds.

5.

11: ASSETS PROTECTION

11.1 Risks to Assets

Your ability to understand and have a full awareness of risks to your assets prepares you to take steps to reduce those risks.

Assets versus Risks

Assets are things you own that have value, while risks are the potential for harm. You can protect the value of your assets by taking steps to reduce the risk exposure. For example, if you have cash on hand, which is an asset, there are risks of potential loss, damages, theft, et cetera. For a homeowner, the risks range from fire or flood to tornado damage, among others.

In order to manage risk exposure to your assets, it is important to understand that you cannot eliminate all risks. There is always potential for harm at any given moment.

You can only eliminate some of them, and/or reduce others in order to keep risk exposure as low as possible.

- Make informed choices that anticipate risks.

- Be careful with personal information as it can be used as a vehicle for potential harm to your assets.

- Know your rights and responsibilities.

- Most importantly, get insurance for your assets whenever it is available.

Insurance is simply a transfer of risks from you to the insurer in exchange for a monthly or annual premium payment.

The insurer promises to pay for covered damages partially or fully as long as you have honored your promise to pay premiums during the life of the contract.

11.2 Insurance

Insurance is one of the most powerful and effective financial **risk management** tools. It provides protection from financial loss. It is recommended to keep accurate records of your assets and any damages to your property. Insurance also reduces the financial impact of a loss or event covered by the insurance policy. It helps protect you from financial catastrophe.

Below are definitions of some of the key terms commonly referred to in insurance contracts.

1. **Insurance Premiums**: This is the amount you pay for your insurance coverage every month or every year depending on the terms of your contract.

2. **Covered Loss:** This is an injury, death, property loss or legal liability, for which an insurance company will pay benefits under the terms of the policy.

3. **Coverage Limit**: The maximum amount of money an insurance company will pay for a covered claim.

4. **Deductible**: A specified amount of money that the insured must pay before an insurance company will pay a claim.

5. **Copayment**: A payment made by a beneficiary, especially for health services, in addition to that made by an insurer.

6. **Coinsurance**: A type of insurance in which the insured pays a share of the payment made against a claim.

7. **Exceptions or Exclusions**: These are situations or circumstances that prevent a beneficiary from receiving insurance benefits. For example, in the case of life insurance, some natures of death may not be covered.

8. **Claim**: This is a formal request to your insurance provider for reimbursement against losses covered under your insurance policy.

9. **Adjudication**: The legal process of resolving a dispute or deciding a claim.

Types of Insurance

You can literally insure anything of value as long as there is a willing insurer who wants to accept the risk transfer. Below is a list of very common types of insurance available in the market worldwide:

1. **Health Insurance**: This is a contract that requires your health insurer to pay some or all of your health care costs in exchange for a premium.

2. **Long-term care insurance**: This is a variety of services designed to meet a person's health or personal care needs during a short or long period of time. These services help people live as independently and safely as possible when they can no longer perform everyday activities on their own.

3. **Dental Insurance**: The coverage that helps pay for the cost of visits to a dentist for basic or preventive services, like teeth cleaning, X-rays, and fillings.

4. **Vision Insurance**: A health benefit that at least partially covers vision care, like eye exams and glasses.

5. **Disability Insurance:** An insurance plan that pays some of a person's income when he or she is disabled from an illness or injury and cannot work.

6. **Life Insurance:** An insurance that pays out a sum of money either on the death of the insured person or after a set period.

7. **Pet Insurance**: A health care policy for your pet that will provide payment or reimbursement for specific health expenses that are covered by the policy.

8. **Identify Theft Insurance**: If your identity is stolen, identity theft insurance helps cover out-of-pocket expenses associated with restoring it. Covered expenses may include legal or administrative fees you need to pay for when restoring your identity.

9. **Vehicle Insurance:** This type of insurance provides coverage for loss or damage to any vehicle such as a car, two-wheeler, or commercial vehicle.

10. **Renter's Insurance**: This is a group of coverages designed to help protect renters living in a house or apartment. A typical renters insurance policy includes three types of coverage that help protect you, your belongings and your living arrangements after a covered loss.

11. **Homeowner's Insurance**: This type of insurance pays for losses and damage to your property if

something unexpected happens, like a fire or burglary.

12. **Flood Insurance**: This covers direct physical loss caused by flood

When you decide to get insurance for your assets, deciding how much coverage you need and the type of policy or rider depends on a number of things:

- Consider your individual circumstances.

- Consider your need to purchase insurance as a tool to manage risks to your assets.

- Consider insuring against things that could happen and cause serious financial harm.

- Some insurances are required by law. For example, in most countries, you must have a vehicle insured before you can drive the vehicle.

- It is important to periodically review your coverage and shop around for better offers.

When you are shopping for insurance coverage:

- Review state-specific information.

- Check out insurance companies.

- Ask about premium discounts to save money.

- Compare several premium quotes.

- Consider the trade-off between deductibles, coinsurance, coverage limits, and premiums.

Keeping Accurate Records

1. It is a very important part of making sure insurance adequately covers your risks.

2. Create and maintain a list of your insured assets.

3. Document any damages and save receipts for related expenses for potential reimbursement by the insurer.

4. File claims as soon as possible.

11.3 Identity Protection

Your biggest and most important asset is your identity. Protecting your identity information is necessary because once jeopardized, it can lead to harming your other assets whether physical, financial, or productive. Every other asset is tied to your identity, therefore, you must protect your identity above all.

You cannot fully eliminate the risk of identity theft unless you live under a rock for the rest of your life. However, there are plenty of measures to minimize the risks of your identity falling into the wrong hands. Your identity is an asset.

Identity theft is a crime that happens when someone uses a person's identifying information without authority.

Identity is any document that has information about your identity. Examples are, among others, your birth certificate, state or national ID, driver's license, passport, and social security number. Identity is also any other information that identity thieves can use to impersonate someone, such as your mailing address, email address, et cetera.

There are several ways in which your identity can be stolen including but not limited to:

- **Phishing**: This happens when someone tricks you into giving your personal information, often through email. *Vishing* is phishing done by phone, while *Smishing* is phishing done by text messages.

- **Spear Phishing**: This is targeted phishing.

- **Pharming**: These are fake websites.

- **Skimming**: This is the act of stealing credit card or debit card numbers.

- **Social media scamming:** This is when someone hacks your social media account.

Warning Signs of Identity Theft

1. withdrawals you didn't make

2. missing bills and statements

3. a merchant refusing your check

4. credit card transaction not going through

5. letters about accounts you didn't open

6. emails about purchases you didn't make

7. statements for credit cards you don't have

8. debt collectors calling you about debts that aren't yours

9. passwords or usernames not working

10. unfamiliar accounts on your credit reports

11. medical bills for services you didn't receive

12. health records for conditions you don't have

13. multiple tax returns or inaccurate tax records

14. notification about data breach

Steps to Minimize Identity Theft

1. Guard your personal information.

2. Don't respond to unsolicited requests.

3. Protect your mail.

4. Sign up for direct deposit.

5. Clean up your financial trash.

6. Review your financial accounts regularly and carefully.

7. Beware of identity theft on the internet.

8. Protect your devices.

9. Review your credit reports at least once every twelve months.

10. Keep your important documents secure.

11. Beware of disaster-related scams.

12. Read scam alerts.

In Case of Identity Theft

The **First Step** to take, should you become a **victim** of identity theft is to work with credit reporting agencies to respond to the theft.

- Place a free fraud alert on your credit report–initial or extended.

- Dispute inaccurate information.

- Consider placing a free credit freeze as well.

The **Second Step** is to communicate with your creditors and debt collectors:

- Alert them about fraudulent accounts.

- Get copies of documents related to the theft of your identity.

- Ask them to stop contacting you about fraudulent accounts.

- Get written information about fraudulent accounts.

The **Third Step** is to know your other federal rights including the fact that you generally have limited liability for fraudulent debts and accounts caused by identity theft.

12: MAKING HOUSING DECISIONS

12.1 Housing Options

There are different types of housing. To help prioritize your options, start by defining what safe and secure housing means for you. You need to decide what features are essential for your housing needs, and then what other amenities you would prefer your house or neighborhood to have. Is it a low crime rate, a good school district for your children, and or a good sense of community?

When it comes to neighborhood choices, what are your needs and wants? For example:

- a safe neighborhood with a low crime rate

- affordable cost of living

- diversity in terms of cultures, ethnics, ages, etc.

- a strong disability community with disability-related services

There are several factors to consider when deciding to rent or buy a house:

- What is the age of the house?

- What is the current housing market and what it is projected to be in a foreseeable future?

- What are current interest rates–especially if you intend to partially finance your house?

- What, if any improvements might your new house need? Will there be repair costs before moving in?

- Is it a neighborhood that you really want?

- Location, location, location.

- What are the amenities and how is the accessibility?

- What is the condition of the house? Look at the wear and tear, given the age of the house.

When you are deciding to buy or rent a house, also ask yourself the following questions:

1. How long do you think you may be staying in the area? Generally, the longer you plan to stay, the more advantages there are to buying a home. Always consider job opportunities and stability, as well as community or family connections. These can affect the amount of time you stay in an area.

2. Do you enjoy home maintenance such as yard work or redecorating? This takes time. The bigger the house or yard, the more time or money it will take to maintain, generally speaking.

3. Options for renting may include renting a room in an apartment or home, renting an apartment, renting a house, getting into subsidized housing, or applying for public housing.

4. Options for buying may include a single-family house, modular home, townhouse, condominium, cooperative (co-op), manufactured home, or mobile home.

12.2 What Can You Afford?

An affordable payment for housing is one you can reliably make each month. So what is affordable? Only you can genuinely decide what is affordable for you. Landlords and mortgage lenders cannot.

There are a number of methods that can help you decide what housing expenses are affordable for you. Methods include the following but not are limited to:

Method One

Annual Gross Income X 3 = Estimate Of Highest Home Purchase Price

For example, if your gross income (income before taxes and other deductions are taken) is $100,000 per year; the highest house you can afford should cost no more than $300,000. Anything more than that is beyond your means, ideally.

This method is helpful when you are looking for a house to buy. However, when calculating your monthly payment, consider other existing and non-recurring expenses in your budget to decide what you can afford to pay monthly. Interest rates also play a major role in this case.

Method Two

Monthly Gross Income X .30 = Estimate of Monthly Housing Cost

This means that if your monthly gross income is $3,000; your monthly housing costs should be around $3,000 X .30 = $900. Sometimes this formula may not be realistic depending on the specific needs of an individual or special circumstances.

Monthly housing costs include items such as rent or mortgage payments, insurance, utilities, maintenance, repairs, et cetera.

Method Three

Total Net Income - Total Non-Housing Expenses = What Is Left For Housing Budget

This works better when you have a solid spending and saving plan. Getting the right net income calculations can be quite tricky sometimes. Whether you receive your income and pay expenses per week, month, quarter, or year, you need to convert your income and expenses to monthly amounts before you can put them into the spending and saving plan.

Then use the plan to help calculate what is left for housing after exhausting other non-housing expenses.

12.3 How To Proceed With Renting

It is important to know ways to protect yourself as a renter. You need to read and understand your rental agreement or lease, get renter's insurance, and know your rights and responsibilities. These are some of the steps to take as you go through the renting process:

1. Decide where you want to live.

2. Decide what kind of place you want to rent.

3. Figure out what you can afford.

4. Understand your credit and how it may affect what you can rent.

5. Research other available options.

6. Get your first month's rent and deposit together.

7. Read and understand your lease or rental agreement.

Step One: Decide where you want to live. Ask yourself what is important to you:

- safety and security

- public transportation lines

- distance to work, childcare, medical services, other needed services, and supportive people

- quality of schools

- access to parks or playgrounds

- accessibility features for people with disabilities

- anything else that is important to you

Step Two: Decide what kind of place you want to rent. Is it a room in an apartment, a full apartment, or a whole house? Keep in mind the following questions:

- Ask if there is a lease requirement.

- Ask how long the lease is, and whether the lease has an employment or school relocation rider which allows you to break it without penalty.

- Ask if the lease allows subletting.

- Make sure your credit is ready in case the landlord wants to check it.

- Be prepared to verify your source of income.

Step Three: What can you afford? Use method 2 or 3, and your spending and saving plan, to decide what you can afford before committing to a lease.

Step Four: Understand your credit and how this may affect what you can rent. Landlords will likely look at your credit reports, and if you have a history of not paying your bills on time, you might even get denied.

If you have a low credit score, or report with negative information, be prepared to:

- spend more time looking for a rental

- have fewer choices of rentals available to you

- pay a large deposit, usually a 3 three-month security deposit

- get a letter of guarantee or someone to cosign

- find roommates to live with you

- reconsider your decision to rent

Step Five: Research Options

You can do it yourself by searching on the internet or renting classified publications. You can also use a real estate agent or ask family and friends if they have any referrals.

Step Six: Get your first month's rent and security deposit together.

- You may have to pay the first month's rent before you move in.

- You will most likely also have to pay a security deposit before you move in and the amount will vary. The security deposit is usually returned to you ten days after you have moved out if you meet the terms of the lease such as no damages, et cetera.

- You will pay other move-in fees upfront.

- Some landlords may require you to purchase renter's insurance.

Step Seven: Read and understand your lease or rental agreement. This is an agreement between you and the landlord or property owner.

For example, it is important to know the names of the parties involved with the lease. This would be the property owner or landlord, you, and anyone else responsible for the rent such as roommates. If roommates are not listed, they will not be held responsible for the rental under your lease. They may have their own lease agreements with the landlord.

The location and description of the rental are also equally important to pay attention to. The description should also name features included such as parking, access to a garage, use of a fitness facility, use of a storage unit, and so on.

Renter's Insurance

It is highly recommended that you have renter's insurance. In some cases, landlords require it. Ask yourself, could you afford to replace your personal property? If a visitor were injured at your residence, could you afford to pay the expenses resulting from the injury?

The purpose of renter's insurance includes the following:

- financial recovery from losses (hazards and disasters are named "perils")

- actual costs or replacement costs

- limited or no coverage for some items

- financial protection from claims of injury at your residence

Know Your Rights as a Renter:

The Fair Housing Act prohibits housing-related discrimination based on race, color, sex, disability, national origin, religion, presence of children, etc.

Also, housing must meet health and safety codes.

You can also request reasonable modifications such as:

- reasonable modifications that residents with disabilities can make and pay for.

- structural modifications to allow full enjoyment of the housing and related facilities such as widening a doorway, lowering kitchen cabinets, replacing flooring, et cetera

You can also request reasonable accommodations such as reserved parking near the entrance for a renter with a disability.

13: BUYING A HOME

13.1. Getting Ready

As you go through the process of a home purchase, it is important to make sure you are doing all you need to do to prepare for buying the home of your dreams. Also, figure out what you can afford. There are several reasons to buy a home such as:

- Building equity: This is the market value of your home minus what you owe on the home, if any. Equity can increase, decrease, or stay the same.

Equity = Home's Market Value - Balance Owed on the Mortgage

There are several factors that affect the market value of a home including the following but not limited to:

1. location

2. current housing supply and demand

3. interest rates

4. macroeconomic environment such as available job opportunities, median income, and unemployment rate

5. the crime rate in the neighborhood

6. school district, etc.

Steps to Buying a Home

Step One: Get Ready

- Decide if you are ready to buy a home.

- Figure out how much you can afford.

- Check your credit history, and clean it up if needed.

Step Two: Get Your Financing Together

- Learn about mortgages or other financing options.

- Shop around for financing options.

- Get pre-qualified or pre-approved.

Step Three: Shop for Your Home

- Put together your support team such as realtors.

- Find a home that fits your needs and that you can afford.

Step Four: Buy Your Home

- Make an offer.

- Negotiate.

- Consider getting a home inspection.

- Close the deal.

Step Five: Maintain Your Home

Always ask yourself the following questions before you commit to buy

1. Do I know why I want to buy a house?

2. Do I have reliable sources of income?

3. Have I received this income on a regular basis for at least the last two or three years?

4. Do I have a credit history?

5. Do I have a good record of paying my bills on time?

There are two ways to estimate how much of a house you can afford to buy. The first option is to review your spending and saving plan. The second is to calculate your Debt-to-Income Ratio.

Method 1: Spending And Saving Plan

Total Net Monthly Income - Total Monthly Non-Housing Expenses = Amount Left For Housing Costs

Ask yourself:

- Can you increase your income?

- Can you decrease your expenses?

- Can you eliminate any expenses?

Bear in mind that the following elements make up part of your monthly mortgage payments:

- **Principal**: the amount you borrowed

- **Interest**: interest on your principal

- **Taxes**: real estate property taxes

- **Insurance**: homeowner's insurance

Bear in mind other additional costs of home ownership including one-time payments such as closing costs, as well as ongoing costs such as landscaping, maintenance, et cetera.

If there is income received on a frequency other than monthly, convert it to monthly before you include it in your plan.

Method 2: Debt-to-Income Ratio

Ratio = Total Monthly Debt Payments/ Total Monthly Gross Income

This shows how much of your monthly gross income (income before taxes or other deductions) goes toward covering your monthly debt payments.

- The higher your debt-to-income ratio, the less money you have to cover these expenses.

- Knowing your debt-to-income ratio before you visit a lender can be quite empowering.

- You can also work to reduce your debt if it seems to be over the limit generally preferred by lenders.

- Use your pay statements or other records of your income to get your gross monthly income.

- Use your monthly bills, loan statements, credit card statements, or other records to get your monthly debt payments.

You should know to the nearest dollar:

- your anticipated monthly housing payment

- your anticipated monthly homeowner or property owner association dues or fees or common area maintenance fees

- your anticipated land rent if you are buying a manufactured or mobile home

- your monthly credit card payments

- your monthly vehicle loan payments

- your monthly personal loan payments

13.2. Financing a Home Purchase

You must know your loan. Learn about your financing options for buying a home and shop around to get the best deal for you. The types of loans available for you will depend on the type of home you are buying.

- For manufactured housing (mobile home) on rented land and/or not on a permanent foundation, you will need a **personal** or **chattel loan**.

- For a unit in a cooperative, you will need a co-op loan or co-op share loan.

- For a house, condominium, or townhouse, you will need a mortgage.

When it comes to mortgages, the following components make up a mortgage contract:

- **Mortgage**: a loan to buy a house

- **Principal**: the amount of money you borrow

- **Costs**: interest, points, fees, other charges

- **Annual Percentage Rate (APR)**: the overall cost of the loan on an annual basis.

A **down payment** is a portion of the house's price you pay in cash. For example, for a 20% down payment requirement, a $200,000 house would require that the buyer pay $40,000 cash, and would need a $160,000 mortgage loan.

The higher the down payment, the less money needed to borrow, and the less the monthly mortgage payment. In some instances where the down payment is less than 20% of the purchase price of a house, **Private Mortgage Insurance (PMI)** may be required by lenders.

- The PMI lowers the risks to the lender.

- It can increase your monthly payments once insurance premiums are included.

Other mortgage characteristics may include loan amount, type of interest rate, loan term, and other upfront costs you must pay at closing. There are two common ways to pay for taxes and insurance:

- Pay them as part of your monthly mortgage payment through an **escrow account**, or at the times required by the lender.

- Pay them yourself directly, which is not as common.

13.3. Types Of Mortgages

There are two major types of mortgage loans. These are **fixed-rate mortgages (FRMs)** and **adjustable-rate mortgages (ARMs)**.

Fixed Rate mortgages:

- have an interest rate that does not change throughout the term of the mortgage

- have a fixed monthly amount unless taxes or insurance in escrow change

- may be a good choice if **interest rates are low**, and if you plan to keep the mortgage for a long time

Adjustable Rate Mortgage:

- may have an initial interest rate that is lower than a fixed rate would be

- adjusts on **predetermined** dates or is tied to an **index**

- may be a good choice if you plan to keep the mortgage for a short time, and you can afford paying more in interest if rates increase and you can't refinance with a lower rate.

It is also important to understand the concept of **rate lock**. In this case:

- Even though mortgage interest rates can change daily, and sometimes hourly, rate lock means your interest rate won't change during the rate lock period.

- Rate lock can be 30, 45, or 60 days, and sometimes longer.

A **balloon** payment is a larger-than-usual one-time payment at the end of the loan term.

Conventional mortgages are the types where you generally need:

- a credit history that lenders consider good

- a regular income

- a debt-to-income ratio within acceptable limits

- a down payment

JUMBO Loan: This is a mortgage above a certain amount of money; usually for relatively expensive homes or homes in high-cost areas.

Second mortgage is typically used to supply additional financing beyond the first mortgage.

Government-guaranteed loans are loans administered and/or promoted by certain government agencies in order to promote equal housing opportunities. Below are examples of some of these Government agencies:

- Federal Housing Administration (FHA)

- US Department of Agriculture (USDA)

- US Department of Veterans Affairs (VA)

- US Department of Housing and Urban Development (HUD)

There is also assistance designed to promote home ownership such as:

- down payment assistance programs

- closing costs assistance programs

- first time home buyer programs

- help for people in specific professions

- loan programs and other programs from your state housing finance agency

The most important elements of a mortgage are the following: the amount of the loan, interest rate, the kind of internal rate (fixed or adjustable), term of the loan (15-year,

30-year, or other), and amortization schedule. The following is a mortgage loan comparison with different Terms:

15-Year Mortgage:

- carries a higher monthly payment

- saves you money in interest over the life of the loan

- will be paid off a lot sooner

30-Year Mortgage

- carries a lower monthly payment

- costs you more in interest over the life of the loan

- will takes longer to pay off

With **amortization**, the amount you pay each month is amortized. The amortization schedule shows how much money from each payment goes toward principal and how much goes toward interest.

As you consider and prepare for your mortgage application, it is a good idea to get pre-qualified or pre-approved.

Pre-qualification will estimate how much money you may be able to borrow. It is not an approval for a loan.

Pre-approval is a commitment from the lender to lend you money under the conditions they specify.

It is recommended that you shop around for a mortgage before you make any commitment to sign up for a loan because shopping around can not only save you money, but also:

- allows you to compare a few loan estimates. A loan estimate is a three page form you receive after applying for a mortgage.

- gives you important details about the loan. You can get one from several lenders. They are free. Make sure you ask any questions you may have.

13.4. Getting Help and Buying Your Home

Get help with the home-buying process. Make sure you conduct a thorough interview and ask for references before you hire help. Understand what services you will receive and how much they will cost. Put together a team made of real estate agents and anyone else who might play a role in helping you buy a home.

A real estate agent will:

- help you find a home that meets your needs and wants

- manage the process of writing your offer on a home and represent you in negotiation with the seller

- manage the process of writing the real estate contract, search the title, and conduct closing with title insurance companies.

You can also select a real estate agent to be your buyer's agent and work on your behalf, not the seller's.

When it is time to make an offer, here is what to expect:

- It can be complicated, but is definitely exciting.

- Your offer basically says "I want to buy your home. And this is how much I am going to pay."

- Your real estate agent or attorney will write your offer.

But first of all, what is an **offer**?

The following are key elements included in an offer:

- address and description of property

- sale price

- the amount of money you are offering

- the target date to pay for closing

- how taxes and utilities will be handled

- who pays for title insurance, termite inspections, property surveys, etc.

- the walk-through clause

- the date the offer expires

- contingencies

- special requests

- other terms

Once you have made an offer, in response, the seller can:

- accept your offer

- reject your offer and make a counteroffer

- reject your offer and not make a counteroffer

Home Inspection

Your home inspection is one of the most important steps in protecting you and your investment. You must conduct an in-depth, unbiased look at the home.

- Evaluate the physical conditions.

- Identify items that need repair or replacement.

- Estimate the remaining useful life of major systems, equipment, structures, and finishes.

Closing

Closing on a home is the most important step in the home-buying process:

- It is the last step.

- The loan becomes final.

- Funds are distributed.

- Congratulations! You own the home.

The following documents are made available at the closing:

- loan estimate

- closing disclosure

- initial escrow statement

- promissory note

- payment option information

- mortgage or security instrument

Like every other financial obligation, your mortgage payment must be met as scheduled. In case you are in financial trouble and are struggling; it is important to get help if you are unable to make your mortgage payments. Contact your lender, the home preservation hotline, a HUD-approved housing counseling agency, or your state housing finance agency.

14: DISASTER PREPARATION AND RECOVERY

14.1. Preparing Financially for Disasters

Save yourself time, money, and stress when a disaster strikes by making financial preparations. Disasters can affect finances in several ways including the following but not limited to:

- cost of meeting immediate needs

- costs of repairing and replacing items

- ongoing costs of items you need

- identity theft

- scams

- access to financial resources

- penalties of missing payments or paying late

Prepare in Advance for Disasters

There are a number of ways of getting prepared financially for disasters. The following are some of the actions you should take to get prepared.

- Get the insurance you need.

- Set money aside in an emergency savings fund.

- Keep some cash in a safe place.

- Sign up for direct deposit.

- Consider online or mobile banking.

- Keep financial documents and information in a safe place.

Get Insurance You Need

Insurance is a support after disasters. Get it before you need it. You should shop around for the best deals possible. Review your policies and know what is covered and what is not covered. Also, make sure you keep records of your personal property. It is important to know what type of insurance could help make you better prepared. The type of insurance coverage should be consistent with the assets you wish to protect or the type of financial risks you wish to mitigate. For example, it could be automobile, disability, life, renter's, or homeowner's insurance, among others.

The cost and coverage vary. Therefore, shop around by using the online option as well as talking with insurance agents. You need to find out what you may need, what it covers, and how much it will cost.

Regarding automobile insurance:

- It can protect you from paying the full cost of repairs to your vehicle in case of an accident.

- Comprehensive coverage helps pay for damages to your vehicle due to theft, fire, or falling objects.

- Depending on the policy, it may cover disaster-related damage.

It is very important to set money aside in an Emergency Savings Fund. As you build an Emergency Savings Fund, it is important to:

- set a realistic goal

- understand that it takes time and commitment

- understand that it is a cycle

- understand that it is worth doing

- understand that it is an important step to improving financial health and stability

Keep Some Cash

Keep some cash in a safe place because cash may be the only option right after a disaster. Keep the cash where you can access it quickly. You may also want to keep it in a larger elegant kit, and make sure that you do not keep more than necessary.

Sign Up for Direct Deposit

- With direct deposit, your paycheck, pension, and public benefits go directly into your account at a financial institution.

- It helps you have access to important income during a disaster.

- If you don't already have an account, you may want to consider one.

Online or Mobile Banking

Your financial institution may be temporarily inaccessible. Therefore, having online or mobile banking would allow you to:

- pay bills

- deposit checks

- conduct other transactions through an online browser or phone app

- communicate with your financial institution

Financial Documents and Information

Keep financial documents and information in a safe place. **Hard copy** records should be kept:

- at home, in a waterproof bag kept in a fire resistant box or safe

- in your Go bag

- in a safe deposit box at a financial institution

- as a scanned copy, emailed securely to yourself

Electronic records must be in a:

- password protected format

- secure offsite data storage service

Keep Records Updated

It is very important to maintain accurate records of important agencies such as their contact addresses and help line numbers. The Federal Emergency Management Agency (FEMA) recommends everyone should have an Emergency Financial Aid Kit (EFAK). www.fema.gov includes checklists and forms to help prepare an EFAK.

14.2. Recovering Financially From a Disaster

Develop an initial plan to recover financially from a disaster. Beware of scams. Make sure you take steps to recover certain properties other than your home, income, expenses, and cash.

Property Other Than Your Home

If you own other property besides your home, make sure you assess the damages on them, if any, and include them in your recovery measures. It is possible to just focus on the immediate issues in your sight, and forget other assets out of sight until it's too late. I recommend you:

- continue making housing payments or contact your lender or landlord

- assess and document damages

- contact your insurance providers

- contact your landlord about damages if you rent

- get help from a HUD-certified housing counseling agency

Income

Amid a disastrous ordeal, it is important to still have money coming in because even when you can not get to work amid a crisis, you still have financial needs and obligations to pay for. Therefore, it is recommended that you:

- contact your employer

- contact your employees benefit provider

- keep track of work days lost

- care for your service animal and repair assistive technology

- contact your disability insurance provider

- explore public benefits, if any

- contact your life insurance provider

- contact schools and financial aid offices

Expenses

Some expenses must be paid amid disasters because they constitute either your obligations or your basic needs for survival. Therefore it is important that you:

- continue paying your bills

- contact the post office to make sure that your incoming bills and your outgoing bill pays are not being held up due to the disaster

- contact your financial institutions

- contact your creditors

- keep records of what you spend

- access assistance programs

Protecting Your Money

Some scammers find the time of disaster and crisis as an opportunity to pull scams on those who are emotionally and physically vulnerable. They may pretend to offer help while collecting your personal information in order to hurt you later. Always make sure you:

- get and review your credit reports

- contact your financial institutions

- contact the department of motor vehicles

- find a safe place for financial information, cash, and other valuables

- contact the post office

Be Proactive

- First, contact the company directly.

- If needed, contact the regulatory agency.

- Consider filing a complaint with the state regulators or attorney general's office.

Get Help

- Visit www.disasterassistance.gov

- Contact the Federal Emergency Management Agency (FEMA) Disaster Recovery Centers.

- Attend locally-organized disaster relief and recovery meetings.

The following are additional financial recovery resources to reach out for help, in addition to starting with www.disasterassistance.gov

- FEMA's Individual and Households Program

- Small Business Administration's low-interest, long-term disaster loans

- Department of Agriculture's disaster loans

- Department of Housing and Urban Development's approved housing agencies

- Home Preservation hotline

Watch Out for Scams

Not everyone who offers help is a legitimate source of help. Be on the lookout for scams and make sure you protect yourself by being cautious. Be selective when accepting help.

To avoid scams:

- Get and check references.

- Ask to see state or local permits.

- Don't pay in full upfront.

- Get and keep receipts.

- Don't pay for services that should be free.

- Research organizations you are not familiar with.

- Protect your information.

- Monitor your credit reports.

- Read Scam alerts and report scams.

Adjust Your Financial Picture After a Disaster

- Take time to grieve and get used to your new reality.

- Review and adjust your spending and saving plan.

- Contact your lenders.

- Contact your financial institution.

- Get ahead and review your credit reports.

- Set new goals and make plans to reach them.

15: FINANCIAL EXPLOITATION

It is important to learn about a spectrum of financial exploitations and frauds against everyday mom-and-pops, older adults, and senior citizens, among others, from all walks of life.

In this chapter, I cover some important points to consider in planning for a more secure financial future as well as how to prepare financially for unexpected life events and disasters. It is important to be able to:

- recognize and reduce the risk of financial exploitation

- guard against identity theft

- plan for possible loss of ability to manage your finances

- prepare financially for disasters

- report financial exploitation

15.1. Understanding Financial Exploitation

Financial exploitation is simply defined as the fraudulent or otherwise illegal, unauthorized or improper action by a caregiver, fiduciary or other individual in which the resources of a person are used by another for personal profit, or improper actions that result in depriving a person of the benefits, resources, belongings, or assets to which they entitled.

Anyone can be a victim of financial exploitation; this issue crosses all social, educational, and economic boundaries. Older adults are at higher risk of financial exploitation because:

- they usually have regular income and have accumulated substantial assets

- they can be too trusting and polite

- they may be lonely and socially isolated

- they may be vulnerable due to grief from the loss of a spouse, family member, friend, or pet

- they can be reluctant to report exploitation by a family member, caregiver, or someone they depend on

- they may receive care from someone with substance abuse, gambling or financial problems, or with other mental health issues.

- they may have fear of retaliation by the exploiter

- they may be unfamiliar with managing financial matters

- they may not have planned the potential loss of a decision-making capacity

- they may be cognitively impaired with diminished ability to make financial decisions or to detect a fraud or scam

- they may be dependent on family members, caregivers, or another person who may pressure them for money or control of their finances.

Some of the examples of financial exploitation include the following but not limited to:

- exploitation by an agent under Power of Attorney or a person in another type of fiduciary relationship

- theft of money or property, often by a family member, caregiver, or in-home helper

- investment fraud and scams, including deceptive "free-lunch" seminars selling unnecessary or fraudulent financial services products

- lottery and sweepstakes scams

- tax and debt collection scams

- charity scams

- scams by telemarketers, mail offers or door-to-door salespersons

- identity theft

- reverse-mortgage fraud

- contractor fraud or home improvement fraud

Most older victims of financial exploitation do not report that they have been financially exploited for a number of reasons including:

- **Shame and embarrassment**: Many people are ashamed to admit that they have been financially exploited.

- **Loyalty**: Some people might be reluctant to report a family member, caregiver, or another person who may treat them well in other ways.

- **Fear of retaliation**: Some older people might fear not being believed or fear losing their independence by being declared incompetent and moved into a *"nursing home."*

- **Dependance:** Victims may be dependent on the abuser for care or assistance.

- **Denial**: Some victims are unwilling or unable to acknowledge that financial exploitation is happening to them.

- **Self-blame:** Abuse can negatively affect an older person's self-esteem, and some victims may believe they deserve or have caused the abuse.

- **Lack of awareness**: Some victims are unaware that they are being exploited, or don't know whom they can report financial exploitation.

There are several types of financial exploitation to be covered; however, below I will give a few examples of the most common ones to be aware of:

15.2. Exploitation by a Fiduciary

A person who is named to manage your money or property is a fiduciary. She or he is bound by the fiduciary responsibility to manage your money and your property in your best interest and benefit. A financial exploitation can occur when a fiduciary abuses that power. Your fiduciary has *four basic duties* including:

1. acting only in your best interest

2. managing your money and property carefully

3. keeping your money and property separate from theirs

4. keeping good records for audit

Your fiduciary can **be removed** if he or she does not fulfill those obligations or duties. Fiduciaries can be sued or may be ordered to repay the money if found to have abused their power. Your fiduciary should be trustworthy and honest.

15.3. Exploitation by Power of Attorney (POA)

Making a power of attorney (POA) for finance is one way some older adults prepare for the possibility of diminished financial decision-making capacity. A power of attorney (POA) gives someone else legal authority to make decisions about money or property. That person, also known as the agent, can make decisions if the beneficiary is sick or injured.

Creating a power of attorney (POA) is a private way to appoint a substitute decision-maker and is relatively inexpensive. If you don't appoint a power of attorney before decision-making ability declines, a family member or friend might have to go to court to have a **guardian** appointed by the court, which can be a lengthy process, expensive, and public.

A power of attorney, however, involves some risks. It gives someone else— your agent— a great deal of authority over your finances without regular oversight, if any.

If abused, the power of attorney can take many forms:

- Your agent may pressure you for authority that you don't want to grant.

- Your agent may spend your money on himself or herself rather than for your benefit.

- Your agent might do things you did not authorize, such as giving gifts or changing beneficiaries on insurance policies or retirement plans.

Depending on your state laws, the Power of Attorney generally goes into effect as soon as it is signed unless the document specifies a different arrangement. That means even if you are still capable of making your own decisions, your agent can immediately act on your behalf.

A **durable** Power of Attorney remains effective even if the grantor loses the capacity to make financial decisions. Otherwise, there are other ways to customize your power of attorney to your needs including making it limited to certain activities or to a timeline.

There are certain ways to minimize the risk of Power of Attorney abuse:

- Trust but verify. Only appoint someone you really trust and make sure they know your wishes and preferences. You can require in your POA that your appointed agent regularly report to another person on the financial transactions he or she makes on your behalf.

- Avoid appointing a person who mismanages their own money or has problems with substance abuse or gambling.

- Tell friends, family members, and financial advisers about your POA so they can look out for you.

- Ask your financial institution about its POA procedures. The financial institution might have its own form that it wants you to complete. However, a POA that is valid under your state's law should be accepted by financial services providers without any further requirement.

- Remember that POA designations can be changed if you decide that your agent is no longer the best person to handle your finances, and you can revoke your POA. Notify all relevant parties including your financial institution if you do this.

A **durable** POA is a very important tool in planning for your financial incapacity due to Alzheimer's disease, other forms of dementia, or other health problems. It is advisable to consult with a lawyer when preparing a **power of attorney, a trust**, or any legal document giving someone else authority over your finances.

15.4. Exploitation by Caregiver and In-home Helpers

Elder financial exploitation is often perpetrated by close family members and other caregivers. Some of the steps to help minimize such exploitation include the following:

- Secure your private financial documents including checks, financial bank statements, and credit cards statements.

- Require receipts for purchases made by helpers.

- Monitor bank accounts and telephone bills. Set up automatic bill payments and turn on transaction alerts on your bank account. Have a family member or other third party do the monitoring.

- Do not let hired caregivers or helpers open your mail, pay your bills, or manage your finances.

- Never promise money or assets or to someone when you die in exchange for care provided now.

- Never lend employees money or personal property.

- If you have trouble reading your financial statements, ask your financial institution to send a second copy to someone else who can read it for you. This person does not need to have authority to act on your behalf.

- Never let caregivers use your credit/debit card to run errands or make purchases for you.

Secure your valuables such as jewelry and other property.

16: FINANCIAL FRAUD

16.1. Investment Fraud

Investment fraud, also known as securities fraud, covers a wide range of illegal investment activities including the deception of investors or the manipulation of financial markets.

Common Types of Investment Scams include:

Ponzi Schemes: This is an old scam (derived from a notorious scammer Mr. Ponzi who built his scamming practice out of Boston in the 1920s) with a simple formula. The scammer promises high returns to investors, much higher than what can realistically be earned in the market on a consistent basis. Money from new investors is used to pay previous investors. These schemes eventually collapse as incoming capital ultimately diminishes while outgoing payments increase with investors' share redemption.

Unscrupulous Stockbrokers: These are financial advisers, also known as brokers, who sell unsuitably high commission investment products in an attempt to make high fees, while leaving investors with bad investment deals.

Affinity Fraud: This is when a scammer pretends to be a member of a religious or military organization in order to win the trust of a member or members of the same group.

Internet Fraud: Scammers often design email and social media business accounts to appear as a legitimate business, in order to ultimately scam investors by selling them fake products.

Fraudulent Annuity Sales: Variable annuities are often pitched through "free lunch investment seminars." These products can be unsuitable to many retirement accounts. Often the salesperson fails to disclose steep sales commissions and annuity surrender charges that impose costly fees or penalties for taking the money out before the annuity maturity date.

It is important to make sure you invest wisely. Here are some tips to keep in mind when considering purchasing investment products and protecting those investments moving forward.

- Never judge a person's trustworthiness by the sound of their voice or their charisma.

- Take your time when making investment choices. Be careful of anyone pressuring you to "act now before it's too late."

- Be wary of investment salespeople who promise returns that sound too good to be true, such as guaranteed high interest rates or no-risk investments.

- Always ask for a written explanation of any investment opportunity, then go shop around and get a second opinion.

- Stay in charge of your money or enlist the help of a trusted and capable third party to assist you.

- Make checks payable to a company or financial institution, never an individual employee.

- Retain and maintain account statements and confirmations about your investment transactions such as stock trades or fund purchase agreements.

- Document every conversation with financial advisers.

- Do not put all of your eggs in one basket. Divide your investments among different asset categories such as stocks, bonds, real estate funds, and cash held in federally insured deposit accounts, money markets, certificates of deposits, etc.

- Take immediate action if you detect a problem. If you cannot reach a settlement through arbitration, do not be afraid to complain to regulators.

- Don't let embarrassment or fear stop you from pursuing losses incurred through investment fraud.

- Do your homework. Never invest in a product you do not understand fully.

- Understand the risks before investing. Investment always has some degree of risk of loss.

- Tell your financial adviser of your investment objectives and risk tolerance.

16.2. Telephone and Internet Scams

IRS Telephone Scams

According to the Internal Revenue Service (IRS), a scammer may call, telling the consumer that he or she must immediately pay taxes that are owed. In most instances, scammers target immigrants who are told that if they don't pay the tax bill or otherwise follow instructions, they will face serious consequences including arrest and deportation.

- They frequently tell potential victims that they are entitled to big refunds, or that they owe money that must be paid immediately to the IRS.

- They usually use common names and surnames to identify themselves and have fake IRS badge numbers.

- They may send bogus IRS emails to victims to support their bogus calls.

- They may create background noise to mimic a call center.

NOTE: The IRS never asks for credit card numbers or debit card information over the phone.

Lottery and Sweepstakes Scams

These scammers may call, email, or text a consumer congratulations on winning a lottery, drawing, or sweepstakes, which the consumer usually has not even entered. The scammer asks the "winner" for an upfront payment to cover processing fees or taxes. Sometimes scammers send a letter with an authentic-looking but phony "claim certificate" or "check" as an advance on the winnings.

Once it is apparent to the victim that no winnings are forthcoming, the victim might receive another call from a person pretending to be an attorney for sweepstakes winners, who also asks for upfront attorney fees in exchange for pursuing the winnings on the victim's behalf. The alleged attorney is usually an accomplice/associate of the original scammer.

NOTE: Below are tips for avoiding telephone scams:

- You usually cannot win a sweepstake or a lottery that you did not enter.

- Never "pay to play." A legitimate sweepstake will not ask for money upfront.

- Be suspicious of any pressure to send funds via wire transfers or prepaid reloadable cards.

- Consider it a red flag if the caller insists on secrecy. Never allow anyone to discourage you from seeking information, verification, support and counsel from family members, friends, or trusted advisers before you make a financial transaction.

16.3. Charity Scam

According to the Federal Trade Commission (FTC), charities and fundraisers (groups that solicit funds on behalf of organizations) use all sorts of communication such as phone calls, emails, or inperson to solicit and obtain donations.

Naturally, scammers use these same methods to take advantage of your goodwill. Always be cautious of any charity or fundraiser that:

- refuses to provide detailed information about its identity, mission, costs, and how the donation will be used

- doesn't provide proof that a contribution is tax deductible

- thanks you for the pledge you don't remember making

- asks for a donation in cash or asks you to wire money

- offers to send a courier or overnight delivery service to collect the donation immediately

- guarantees sweepstakes winnings in exchange for a contribution. By law, you never have to give a donation to be eligible to win a sweepstakes

The following tips will help you minimize being a victim of a charity scam, while keeping your goodwill going.

First, ask if the caller is a paid fundraiser. If so, ask the name of the charity they represent, the percentage of your donation that will go to the charity, how much will actually go to the cause you are supporting, and how much will go to the fundraiser.

Second, keep a record of your donations.

Third, make an annual donation plan. That way you can decide which causes to support and which reputable charities should receive your donations.

Fourth, know the difference between "**tax exempt**" and "**tax deductible**." Tax exempt means the organization doesn't have to pay taxes. Tax deductible means you can deduct your donation contribution on your federal income tax return.

Fifth, never send cash donations. For security and tax purposes, it is best to pay by check—make it payable to the charity–or pay by credit card.

Sixth, do not donate until you have thoroughly researched the charity.

Seventh, be wary of charities that spring up suddenly in response to current events and natural disasters. Even if they are legitimate, they might not have the infrastructure in place to get the donation to the affected area or people.

NOTE: If you think you have been a victim of a charity scam, you can file a complaint with the Federal Trade Commission (FTC).

17: PLANNING FOR UNEXPECTED

LIFE EVENTS

Planning ahead for any unexpected life events before they happen is very important. The last thing you want is to think about making plans when it is too late to act. Advance planning gives you control and options for your situation.

- It takes the stress of decision-making from caretakers and family members.

- It saves money and helps you avoid financial disasters or setbacks.

- It allows time for gathering information, comparing options, and determining which options help achieve what is most important.

17.1. Long-Term Care

The majority of people who need long-term care are senior citizens. However, the need for long-term care can come at any age due to *disability, chronic diseases, accidents, brain injuries, strokes, and other debilitating events.*

Families and individuals who plan ahead for a disability will be in a better position to cope in the event of a disability. Consider taking these steps before you or a family member becomes ill or disabled.

- Prepare a plan by reviewing your income and expenses.

- Make sure trusted family members know where to find personal and financial documents in an emergency.

- Set up direct deposit for income and benefit checks such as social security or pension into a savings account, etc.

- Consider setting up automatic payment of important recurring bills.

- Consider a durable power of attorney, which gives one or more people authority to handle finances and remains in effect if you become incapacitated.

- Make sure you are properly insured. Speak with your financial planner or an insurance agent you trust. Review your insurance policy regularly because your needs can change.

- Maintain a healthy lifestyle.

You should always have the following documents, bank products, and other items in a secure place and readily available in a case of emergency:

- For identification, you should always have your driver's license, insurance cards, social security card, passport, and birth certificate ready and reachable by your trusted agent.

- Keep a checkbook with enough blank checks and deposit slips to last at least three months.

- It is advisable to maintain some emergency cash on hand.

- Keep a list of telephone numbers for your financial services providers.

- All your important account numbers should be kept safe but readily accessible. These include: bank and brokerage account numbers, credit card numbers, and insurance policy numbers.

- The key to your safe deposit box should be kept by a trusted family member.

After you have gathered your most important financial items and documents, protect them as well as you can while also ensuring you have access to them in case of emergency.

Make backup copies of important documents:

- Give a copy of your documents to loved ones or let them know where to find the documents in an emergency.

- Store your backups at some distance from your home in case a disaster impacts your entire community.

Most importantly, seal important documents in airtight and waterproof plastic bags or containers to prevent water damage.

Prepare one or more emergency evacuation bags. Pack essential financial documents such as cash, checks, copies of your credit cards (front and back), and a key to your safe deposit box. Make sure each evacuation bag is waterproof and easy to carry. Keep it in a secure place in your home.

17.2. Other Life Events

Prepare for other events such as **mental incapacitation** or **death** by making sure you have a **living will** written–a **medical directive** expressing your wishes, in case someone has to make medical decisions for you, including the decision to cease life support.

You should sit down with a financial planner to make sure you have enough life insurance coverage to take care of your funeral cost, pay your debts and leave something behind for your surviving loved ones. For example, money to cover tuition for your kids, if any. An experienced financial planner or a trust attorney can help you with all estate planning needs including setting up a trust in your legacy.

18: RETIREMENT PLANNING

It is never too early or too late to start thinking about saving for retirement. Retirement planning is an ongoing process. Each plan is unique, but everyone should make one. The sooner, the better.

18.1. Getting Started

It is hard to save for retirement when you have other financial concerns; but if you break it down into manageable steps it will seem a lot easier. The following are some ideas to help you get started:

1. **Make saving a habit.** Decide how much you can set aside in your monthly budget toward your retirement savings, and stick to your goal. Consider making automatic contributions. Contact your bank or financial institution to find out how.

2. **Explore ways to save**. How much you save and spend are the most important factors in achieving your retirement goals–even more important than how you invest. Look at your expenses and determine where you can cut back and how you can save more.

3. **Make the most of tax-advantaged retirement accounts.** Investing in a tax-advantaged account, such as an Individual Retirement Account (IRA)—or a 401(k) if available through your work—allows your earnings to grow tax-free, so that even small contributions can become more significant over time.

18.2. Types of Retirement Accounts

There are several types of retirement savings options and retirement accounts available. Below are some common ones.

- **Individual Retirement Accounts (IRAs):** **Traditional IRAs** and **Roth IRAs** are popular retirement accounts that individuals can contribute to. Contributions to traditional IRAs may be tax-deductible, while Roth IRA contributions are made with after-tax money.

- **401(k) Plans**: These are employer-sponsored retirement plans where employees can contribute a portion of their salary. Some employers may match a percentage of the employee's contributions.

- **403(b) Plans**: Similar to 401(k) plans, 403(b) plans are offered to employees of certain tax-exempt organizations, such as schools, hospitals, and non-profit organizations.

- **Simplified Employee Pension (SEP) IRA**: This retirement account is available to self-employed individuals and small business owners. Contributions to a SEP IRA are made by the employer on behalf of the employee.

- **Savings Incentive Match Plan for Employees (SIMPLE) IRA**: This retirement plan is designed for small businesses with fewer than 100 employees. Both employers and employees can make contributions to the account.

- **Pension Plans:** These retirement plans are typically provided by employers and offer a fixed benefit to employees after they retire. Pension plans have become less common in recent years.

18.3. Retirement Contributions Limits

As of 2024, contribution limits, which can change over time, are the following:

- For IRAs (Traditional and Roth): The annual contribution limit is $7,000 (or $8,000 if you're age 50 or older).

- For 401(k) and 403(b) Plans: The annual contribution limit is $23,000 (or $26,000 if you're age 50 or older).

- For SEP IRAs and SIMPLE IRAs: The contribution limits vary. For SEP IRAs, it's typically the lesser of 25% of compensation or $58,000. For SIMPLE IRAs, the limit is \$13,500 (or \$16,500 if you're age 50 or older).

18.4. Retirement Planning Steps

1. Decide what you want to do in retirement. It is recommended that you write down your top five goals, and be realistic and practical.

2. Take stock of what you have. Don't think only about money. Think about your skills and hobbies, too. These help you enjoy life—and sometimes you can use them to earn money in retirement.

3. Evaluate your health. Schedule check ups and preventive exams. Eat healthy, exercise, and get enough sleep. Staying in close contact with nurturing family and friends will help you maintain your health physically and mentally.

4. Decide when to collect social security. The longer you wait to collect social security (generally until age 70), the more money you will receive each month.

5. Network. Building your network can help you find opportunities and perhaps a job. Do you enjoy using social media? If so, staying in touch through social media platforms, especially LinkedIn, can help you build social and professional relationships. If not, be socially active with friends and organizations.

6. Decide about a retirement job. Whatever your main reason for working— money, social connections, interests— don't wait until after retirement to make a decision about your employment prospects during retirement. The sooner you are comfortable with your decision, the better you can prepare.

7. Create a retirement budget. As you track income and expenses, think about whether you will be able to

manage with less in retirement— or not— and plan accordingly.

8. Cut expenses any way you can and spend wisely will help you save more for retirement.

9. Prepare for the unexpected. Don't get caught off guard. Consider how you would pay for an extended illness, home repairs, or some other emergency, and put money aside. Make sure the amount is adequate.

10. Stick to your plan. Get the support of friends, family, your network, or your money mentor to help you stay on track.

18.5. Retirement Withdrawal Guidelines

The guidelines provide recommendations on how much money you can safely withdraw from your retirement savings each year to ensure your funds last throughout your retirement. These numbers are based on historical retirement data with consideration of 62 years old as the median retirement age. Below are the three most commonly followed withdrawals guidelines:

1. **The 4% Rule:** This guideline suggests withdrawing 4% of your retirement savings in the first year and adjusting subsequent withdrawals for inflation. It is based on historical data and is designed to provide a high likelihood of sustaining your savings for 30 years.

2. **Required Minimum Distributions (RMDs):** RMDs are mandatory withdrawals from traditional retirement accounts (e.g., 401(k)s and IRAs) that begin at age 72. The amount is calculated based on your account balance and life expectancy, as determined by IRS guidelines.

3. **Flexible Withdrawal Strategies:** Some financial advisors recommend adjusting your withdrawal rate based on market conditions and your personal financial situation. In bear markets, you may withdraw less to preserve your savings, while during good market conditions, you can withdraw more.

NOTE: It's important to understand that these guidelines are not universal and may not suit everyone's circumstances. Factors like your retirement goals, portfolio allocation, health, and other income sources should also be considered. Consulting a financial advisor can help tailor a withdrawal strategy that aligns with your specific needs.

19: ESTATE PLANNING

19.1. Living Will

A living will, also known as an advance directive, is a legal document that allows you to outline your healthcare preferences and decisions in the event you become unable to communicate or make decisions for yourself.

It specifies the medical treatments or interventions you wish to receive or decline if you are incapacitated or unable to make decisions. It typically addresses end-of-life care and situations where you are in a terminal condition or a persistent vegetative state.

- **Advantages of a Living Will**

There are many advantages to, and reasons for, having a written living will in place. Some of the examples are the following:

- **Ensuring Personal Wishes**: It enables you to have control over your medical care and ensures that your wishes are honored when you cannot communicate your preferences.

- **Reducing Family Conflict**: By clearly stating your healthcare decisions, a living will can help prevent disagreements and conflicts among family members who may have differing opinions about medical treatments.

- **Alleviating the Burden on Loved Ones**: Having a living will relieve the burden on family members or loved ones, as they won't have to make difficult decisions on your behalf if you are incapacitated.

Steps to Establishing a Living Will

1. **Research**: Understand the laws and requirements regarding living wills in your jurisdiction.

2. **Decision-making**: Reflect on your healthcare preferences and consider various scenarios and treatments you would want or decline.

3. **Consultation**: Talk to your physician, lawyer, or a professional experienced in healthcare directives to gain clarity and guidance.

4. **Drafting**: Prepare the living will document, ensuring it is clear, specific, and in compliance with legal requirements.

5. **Witnesses and Signatures:** Typically, living wills require witnesses or notarization. Follow the guidelines in your jurisdiction to ensure validity.

6. **Distribution**: Provide copies of the living will to your healthcare provider, family members, and anyone else involved in your care.

7. **Review and Update**: Periodically review your living will to ensure it aligns with your current wishes, and make revisions as needed.

19.2. The Will

This is a legal document that expresses your wishes regarding the distribution of your assets and the care of any dependents after your death. It serves as a crucial tool for estate planning.

The Will outlines how your property, possessions, and assets should be distributed upon your death. It may also address other important matters such as the appointment of guardians for minor children and the naming of an executor to carry out the instructions in the will.

Advantages of Having a Will

- **Asset Distribution**: A will allows you to specify how your property and assets should be distributed among your chosen beneficiaries, ensuring your wishes are followed.

- **Guardianship of Dependents:** If you have minor children, a will allows you to designate a guardian who will care for them in the event of your passing.

- **Executor Appointment**: You can name an executor in your will, someone you trust to handle the administrative tasks of managing your estate and distributing assets.

- **Avoiding Intestacy Laws**: Without a will, your estate will be distributed according to state intestacy laws, which may not align with your wishes.

- **Minimizing Family Disputes:** A clear and well-drafted will can help reduce conflicts and disagreements among family members regarding asset distribution.

Steps to Establishing a Will

1. **Determine your assets**: Make a list of all your assets, including property, investments, bank accounts, and personal belongings.

2. **Choose beneficiaries**: Decide who you want to inherit your assets and in what proportion.

3. **Appoint an executor**: Select a trustworthy person to carry out the instructions in your will and handle your estate.

4. **Consult an attorney:** Seek legal advice from an attorney who specializes in estate planning to ensure your will is valid and properly executed.

5. **Draft your will**: Work with your attorney to create a clear and comprehensive will that reflects your wishes.

6. **Execute the will**: Sign your will in the presence of witnesses, as required by your jurisdiction's laws.

7. **Store your will safely**: Keep your original will in a secure location and inform your executor or a trusted family member of its whereabouts.

8. **Review and update**: Regularly review and update your will to account for any changes in your

circumstances, such as births, deaths, or changes in assets.

19.3. Trust Funds

A trust fund is a legal arrangement where one party, known as the **grantor**, transfers assets to a **trustee** who holds and manages those assets for the benefit of another person or group of people, known as the **beneficiaries**. Trust funds are commonly established for various purposes, including estate planning, charitable giving, and providing financial security for loved ones.

Types of Trust Funds:

Revocable Living Trust: This type of trust allows the grantor to maintain control over the assets during their lifetime and to make changes or revoke the trust if desired.

Irrevocable Trust: Once an irrevocable trust is established, it cannot be altered or revoked without the consent of the beneficiaries. This type of trust offers certain tax advantages and asset protection benefits.

Charitable Trust: These trusts are created with the intention of benefiting a charitable organization or cause. They can provide both tax benefits and the satisfaction of supporting a charitable purpose.

Special Needs Trust: This trust is designed to provide financial support and care for individuals with special needs, ensuring they receive necessary services without affecting their eligibility for government benefits.

Spendthrift Trust: A spendthrift trust is created to protect the assets from being mismanaged or quickly depleted by a financially irresponsible beneficiary. It provides ongoing financial support while protecting the assets from creditors.

The Advantages of Trust Funds

- **Asset protection:** Trust funds can safeguard assets from creditors, lawsuits, and potential financial risks.

- **Control and flexibility**: Trusts allow grantors to determine how and when their assets will be distributed to beneficiaries, ensuring the funds are used according to their wishes.

- **Privacy**: Unlike wills, which go through probate and become public record, trust funds offer privacy since they are generally not subject to probate proceedings. *Probate* is a formal legal process that gives recognition to a will and appoints the executor or personal representative who will administer the estate and distribute assets to the intended beneficiaries.

- **Tax benefits**: Depending on the type of trust and local tax laws, trust funds may offer tax advantages, such as reducing estate taxes or capital gains taxes.

Steps To Establishing a Trust Fund

1. **Determine the purpose**: Clearly define the purpose of the trust, such as providing for family members, charitable giving, or protecting assets.

2. **Choose a trustee**: Select a trustworthy individual, corporate entity, or professional trustee who will be responsible for managing the assets and carrying out the terms of the trust.

3. **Identify beneficiaries**: Determine who will benefit from the trust and specify their rights and entitlements.

4. **Draft the trust document**: Consult with an attorney to create a legally binding trust document that

outlines the terms, conditions, and instructions for the trust.

5. **Fund the trust**: Transfer assets into the trust, which may include cash, property, investments, or other valuable assets.

6. **Execute the trust**: Sign the trust document and ensure it complies with all legal requirements.

7. **Maintain the trust**: Regularly review and update the trust as needed to reflect any changes in circumstances or preferences.

Disclaimer

It is important to note that:

- Information provided in this chapter about trusts, living will, and the will is a general overview, and it's important to consult with an attorney or financial advisor who can provide personalized guidance based on your specific situation.

- Laws regarding wills may vary across jurisdictions, so it's important to consult with a qualified professional to ensure compliance with local regulations.

- Specific laws and procedures regarding living wills may vary depending on your jurisdiction, so it's advisable to seek legal advice or consult local resources when creating a living will.

20: ACTION PLAN

This is where you tie together everything you have learned in this book and apply them to your day-to-day management of your personal finances. Think about the goals you want to achieve. Refer to your goal-setting notes. Some will remain the same over time, others evolve as time and circumstances call for it.

Think about what matters most to you, and how improving your financial situation can help you achieve your life goals. **This is where you want to go.**

Think about how improving your credit, managing your debt, and building savings can help you achieve your overall financial and personal goal; then write down the steps you will take. **This is how you will get there.**

As time passes, you can track your progress, striving toward meeting your deadlines as you cross items off your "To-Do" list. You will see that your road map is leading closer and closer to where you want to be.

20.1. Action One: Six Tips For Getting Organized

Getting your finances organized is the first step to getting them under control. Once you know where to store and find important documents and bills, you will feel better prepared for budgeting and saving. Below are some helpful suggestions:

1. Check your budget at least once a month and adjust expenses if necessary as bills come in.

2. Contact your bank about automatic bill-pay, which can help you keep track of your bills, and transfer money between accounts if necessary to cover a bill. Alternatively, keep all your unpaid bills in one place and note due dates on your calendar. Check your balance regularly to make sure there are no unexpected charges on your account.

3. Set up a filing system with one or more separate files for household accounts such as mortgage or rent payment statements, income such as pay stubs and benefit statements, savings and check accounts, credit cards and department store cards, other debts, retirement and investment accounts, tax returns for each of the last years, and a net worth worksheet.

4. Keep insurance policies, wills and trusts, birth and marriage certificates, passports and other hard to replace documents in a fireproof safe box. If you have a computer, keep a backup copy of the financial records in a password protected area or a separate drive.

5. Look into online record-keeping. Many of your records may already be available online, particularly bank and investment accounts.

6. Shred sensitive documents such as paid bills, old bank statements, old investment statements once they are no longer needed.

20.2. Action Two: Things To Remember When You Can't Pay Your Bills

1. Prioritize your debts. If there would be serious consequences for not paying a bill such as losing your car or house, make sure you keep up with your payments or talk to your lender.

2. Budget for getting out of debt. Stick to your budget, and try to include realistic amounts you can pay off each month.

3. Seek help immediately. Be willing to accept help when offered. If you feel you need a lawyer, find out if there is free legal aid in your community.

4. Talk to your creditors. Let them know your situation. Some might agree to a payment plan or to restructuring your debt.

5. Consider reputable credit counseling. A reputable credit counselor can help you sort out your debt and start creating a repayment plan. Look for a local non-profit counseling service by contacting the National Foundation for Credit Counseling, 1-800-388-2227 or visit www.nfcc.org

6. Watch out for scams. Credit repair agencies are generally not worth the money. They may claim to repair your credit but they will most likely charge you for things you could do yourself.

7. Avoid "debt relief" or " debt settlement" companies. These services typically charge high fees without really relieving you of the debt or changing the circumstances or habits that led to it. In addition, your use of such services might be noted on your credit report. A debt management plan with a reputable credit counseling agency is a better choice. However,

reputable and legitimate debt consolidation may be an option.

8. Consider the **pros** and **cons** of bankruptcy. The bankruptcy process is complicated; and it does not eliminate certain kinds of debt. But as a very last-resort option, it may be worth looking into different types of bankruptcies to determine if any would help your situation. A nonprofit credit counseling agency or attorney may be able to help you look into it.

9. If a debt collector calls, be sure you know your rights. There are limits to what debt collectors can do or say. For example, they may not contact you at unreasonable times, harass you, or make false or misleading statements.

For more information, visit the Consumer Finance Protection Bureau (CFPB) at www.consumerfinance.gov. The CFPB has information about mortgage help that includes a list of foreclosure prevention resources by state, as well as a list of legal aid by state.

20.3. Action Three: Reading Credit Card Agreements and Disclosures

Every credit card comes with an agreement that clearly spells out the interest rates, fees, and penalties charged by the card, as well as your consumer rights and the process of disputing charges. It is important to keep a copy of your credit card agreements so that you understand how much interest each credit card charges, how to avoid triggering penalties, and so on. But if you don't have a copy, here is a list of what to look for:

1. Check the real interest rate or annual annual percentage rate (APR) for purchases beyond the

introductory rate because the introductory rate can quickly go up.

2. Find out if there is an annual fee.

3. Compare late fees and "over credit limit" fees. When you first get a card, the credit limit is probably fairly low. Therefore it is probable that you may go over your limit before you know what happened. Late fees may increase as your balance goes up.

4. Read details of the default rate, which is the rate charged if you miss payments. These can be as high as 30%.

5. Compare **grace periods**. This is the time you have after making a purchase to paying for it without having to pay interest.

6. Expect changes to your fees as time goes on. The small print probably tells you that "rates, fees, and

terms of this account are subject to change at any time, for any reason."

7. While prizes, points, and rebates are nice, do not make them your main reason for choosing one card over another. They may encourage you to spend more.

20.4 Action Four: Understand Your Credit Reports

Your credit report says a lot about you and what it says can help or hurt you. A high score can help you get better interest rates. A low score can keep you from getting certain jobs, loans, or lower interest rates. It is important to monitor your credit report so that you can dispute any errors and identify problems you need to correct.

By law, each one of the three main credit reporting agencies— Experian, Equifax, and TransUnion—is required to provide you with your credit report free of charge once per year. To stay up to date, consider requesting a free report from one agency every four months on a rotating basis. You can also get a report from all three by contacting www.annualcreditreport.com or by calling 1-877-322-8228. This is the only authorized one-stop source of the annual credit report for all three bureaus. Watch out for scam companies that claim they are the one-stop source.

20.5. Action Five: Credit Protection— Know Your Rights

Many federal laws protect your rights when you interact with your credit card company. For example, these laws protect you by:

1. requiring that you be told clearly about fees and interest rates

2. limiting fees and rates increases

3. prohibiting discrimination in availability of credit

4. requiring that mistakes on your bill be corrected without damaging your credit score

5. allowing you to dispute errors in your credit file

6. limiting your liability to $50 if your credit card is lost, stolen, or used without your permission.

20.6. Action Six: What To Do If Your Identity Is Stolen

Identity theft can wreak havoc with your finances, credit history, and reputation. And it can take time and patience to resolve. According to the Federal Trade Commission (FTC), acting quickly is the best way to limit the damage. The FTC recommends four steps if your identity is stolen.

1. Place a fraud alert on your credit reports, and review your reports. To place a fraud alert, contact any one of the three main credit reporting agencies. That agency in turn informs the others on your behalf. This makes it harder for anyone to get any more access in your name. Once you place a fraud alert, you can order a free report from each agency.

2. Close the account that you know or believe has been tampered with, used, or opened fraudulently.

3. File a report with the police in your local community or in the community where identity theft took place.

4. File a complaint with the FTC. You can file a complaint online by visiting www.ftc.gov

GLOSSARY: KEY DEFINITIONS

401(k) Plan: A defined contribution plan in which an employer takes money directly from an employee's salary and places it in a tax-deferred retirement account. The employee doesn't pay taxes on this money until he or she withdraws it. Employers often match a percentage of employee contributions.

Annual Fee: A charge imposed each year for using a credit card. It may also be a membership or participation fee.

Annual Percentage Rate (APR): The cost of credit on a yearly basis, expressed as a percentage of the loan amount.

Annual Percentage Yield (APY): The amount paid on the principal of an interest-bearing investment or account in a year, expressed as a percentage (or growth interest rate).

Asset: A property that has monetary value, including personal possessions (such as house, cars, and jewelry) and financial assets (for example, savings and investment accounts).

Asset Allocation: How your assets are divided among stocks, bonds, real estate, and cash. These basic asset classes respond to the market differently–when one is up, another can be down. Asset allocation is a key to investing success. Also known as asset mix.

Bankruptcy: A legal process that helps consumers and businesses get rid of debts and repay their creditors. There are different types of bankruptcy. Because it affects future credit and because bankruptcy does not eliminate some debts, it is a last-resort option.

Bond: A type of investment that is similar to an IOU from a corporation, or a municipal or federal government. Money is loaned, with interest, for repayment in full on a specific date.

Budget: A plan that estimates income and expenses in order to achieve financial goals.

Certificate of Deposit (CD): An FDIC-insured investment made with a financial institution in which a specific amount is deposited for a specific period of time, at a preset, fixed interest rate.

Credit Builder Loan: A loan designed to help improve one's credit report. Loans are typically for small amounts and generally involve giving a lender money upfront or in regular payment over a period of time.

Credit Bureau: A company that collects and sells information about how people handle credit. The reports are made available to individuals and to creditors who profess to have a legitimate need for information. The three major national credit bureaus are Equifax, Experian, and TransUnion.

Credit Card: A card that allows a person to purchase goods and services by paying with money borrowed from a creditor. The borrower then repays the credit card company, often with interest. There is usually a grace period before interest is charged on a new purchase.

Credit Counseling: Personal financial services that include budget counseling and education, debt management, and financial literacy courses.

Credit Report: A document containing financial information about a person, focusing on his or her history of paying obligations, such as mortgages, car payments, utility bills, and credit cards. It also includes the current balance on outstanding debts, the individual's amount of available credit, public records such as bankruptcies, and inquiries about credit from various companies.

Credit Score: A three-digit number that reflects the credit history detailed by a person's credit report.

Debit Card: A card that allows an individual to transfer funds instantly from a bank account.

Debt: An amount owed by an individual, a corporate entity, or a government agency.

Debt Consolidation: The process of taking out one loan to pay off many others, often to secure a lower interest rate or for the convenience of paying only one loan.

Disclosure Box: Also called fee disclosure box. The standardized disclosure box appears on credit card applications and features relatively consistent terms and conditions for credit card offers so that consumers can compare cards.

Diversification: Lowering risk potential by spreading money across and within different asset classes such as stocks, bonds, and cash equivalents.

Earned Income Tax Credit: A tax credit for low-income workers who meet certain requirements, and have earned income considering specific limits. Even workers whose income is too small to have paid taxes may qualify for the earned income credit.

Federal Deposit Insurance Corporation (FDIC): A government entity that insures deposits in banks and thrift institutions, assuring bank customers that their savings and checking accounts are safe. As of 2024, coverage is up to $250,000 per depositor per bank for individual, joint, and trust accounts. Business accounts are also insured.

Finance Charge: The charge for using a credit card, including interest costs and other fees.

Grace Period: The period during which you are charged and allowed to pay your credit card bill without having to pay interest. The grace period usually applies only to new purchases. Most credit cards do not give a grace period for cash advances and balance transfers–instead, interest charges start right away.

Home Equity: The difference between a home's current appraisal and what you owe on it. For example, if your home is worth $500,000 and you owe $300,000; your equity is $200,000.

Home Equity Loan: A loan based on the amount of equity a homeowner has in the property. The interest paid on a home equity loan may be tax deductible. It is different from a home equity line credit. A home equity loan features a fixed rate payment and term, usually five to fifteen years.

Identity Theft: The unauthorized use of your personal information such as your name, address, social security number, or credit account information.

Individual Retirement Account (IRA): IRAs are retirement accounts with tax advantages. You may contribute up to the limit of each taxable year. Or, if you are age 50 or older, you can put aside more. But your contributions can't exceed your earned income. The investment growth is not taxed until you begin making withdrawals, usually after age 59.5. Before then, if you take money out, you will usually face a 10% penalty and pay taxes on the amount withdrawn.

Installment Credit: A type of credit in which the monthly payment is the same every month and the loan has a set time period. The most common forms of installment credit are mortgages and auto loans.

Interest Rate: A percentage the borrower must pay in addition to the amount borrowed. Generally, interest rates are higher when the risk is greater for the lender.

Invest: To put money into something (such as stocks or mutual funds) with the hope of achieving a profit.

Investment Account: Also known as a brokerage account, an investment account allows you to invest in a wide variety of securities including stocks, bonds, mutual funds, and fixed-income products.

Liability: An obligation to make a payment or settle a debt (for example, a mortgage or car loan payment).

Minimum Payment: The minimum amount a cardholder must pay to keep the account from defaulting. Often, this amount is at least 2% of the outstanding balance.

Money Market Account: A bank deposit account that permits a limited number of cash transactions per month and typically pays interest at rates similar to or slightly below the rate on short term Certificates of Deposit (CDs). You can take your money out at any time and earn interest until you withdraw it. Like bank products, money market accounts have the safety of Federal Deposit Insurance Corporation (FDIC) protection.

Mortgage: A form of debt in which one can own a property by paying the entire price over time with interest— typically a loan to buy a house.

Mutual Fund: A type of investment that pools the money of many investors to buy various stocks, bonds, and/or cash equivalents.

Needs: Necessary expenses, or must-haves, such as your mortgage or rent, groceries, and transportation.

Net Worth: A person's or entity's value, calculated by subtracting what is owed (liabilities) from what is owned (assets).

Overdraft Protection: It ensures that all checks you write and electronic transactions you authorize will clear, even if you spend more than the balance in your account. If you link a savings account to a checking account or qualify for an overdraft line of credit, money is transferred from that account or line of credit to cover the shortfall. You pay interest if you use your line of credit.

Portfolio: The collection of investment assets you hold is called your investment portfolio.

Predatory Lenders: Lenders who take advantage of borrowers by employing a variety of deceptive financial practices. They may ask for money upfront, charge very high interest rates or excessive fees, steer borrowers into larger loans, hide costs, or use high pressure tactics.

Prepaid Debit-Card: Often compared with an electronic bank account, the card is loaded with a specific amount of money that is prefunded (or paid for) in advance. You can pay for things with a debit card without carrying cash around. Some cards must be used in a particular store for a limited amount of money. Other cards can be used anywhere that accepts the card's payment network (such as Mastercard or Visa). Some cards are reloadable, meaning you can add money to them.

Reverse Mortgage: A special type of home loan that lets you convert part of the equity in your home into cash.

Revolving Credit: An account that requires a minimum payment each month plus service charges on the remaining balance. As the balance declines, so does the service charge. The most common examples are credit cards and store cards.

Secured Debt: Debt that is attached to something tangible. Common examples of secured debt are mortgages and auto loans. If you fail to repay secured debt, you could lose the item attached to it. For example, if you do not pay your car loan, your car may be repossessed.

Social Security: America's earned benefit program for workers who worked in social security-covered employment, and for their families. Payroll taxes from employers and employees pay for the benefits.

Stock: In investing terms, stock is a share or shares of ownership of a company; and individuals usually purchase them (invest in them) in hopes of gaining a profit. There are many types of stocks.

Unsecured Debt: Unsecured debt isn't attached to any kind of property or product. Common examples of unsecured debt are credit cards, medical bills, and store cards, where you do not have to put up any materials as security for the debt. The debt is granted based on the full faith of your credit worthiness.

Wants: Expenses that are nice to have but not essential, such as entertainment, travel, and new clothing.

INFORMATION RESOURCES AND

REFERENCES

Based on my own information and data references in preparation of this book, more information is available on the resources below:

1. AARP Money at www.aarp.org/money for tips and essays related to personal finance

2. Consumer Financial Protection Bureau at www.consumerfinance.gov, for more information about credit, debt, and asset protection

3. Elder Financial Protection Network at www.bewiseonline.org; for information about protecting your money

4. Federal Trade Commission (FTC) at www.ftc.gov; for consumer protection inquiries

5. Financial Literacy and Education Commission at www.mymoney.gov; plenty of information about a wide range of financial topics

6. National Endowment for Financial Education at www.smartaboutmoney.org; for guidance on how to manage retirement income

7. Non-Profit Credit Counseling Services. Find a local resource at www.nfcc.org or call 1-800-388-2227

8. Social Security Administration at www.ssa.gov; for social security benefits related information

9. Your local public library

10. Federal and State housing agencies for information about affordable housing and mortgage payment assistance programs